THE ISLANDS OF SEDANIA

Volume 2
A Pirate's Bargain
L.C. Owen

DEDICATION

I dedicate this book to every woman who has ever attempted to navigate the world as a single mom. Your job is thankless. Your road is long. Somehow, through it all, you've managed to juggle the many pressures of life.

ACKNOWLEDGMENTS

As I sit on the porch of our vacation rental on the beach, I am reminded at how truly blessed my life has been. I can feel the breeze on my cheeks. The warm sun shines down on my skin. The soothing sound of ocean waves moving to and fro on the sandy beach are singing their lullaby. I never thought I'd be sitting here watching my boys grow in the summer sun while they played in the dancing waves. As my thoughts have tossed about in my mind over the years, finally getting it all in print is a dream come true. Life has given me many experiences to draw from. Those along the way have inspired and encouraged me to this place of bliss. I thank my wonderful parents Bill and Toni for teaching me to be diligent in my efforts, never to quit, and to love unconditionally. I also thank my dear step-mom Julie for taking a hand in raising me and giving me her heart by choice. To my ex-husband Andrew and his wife Christy, thank you for sharing in the joy of raising our two sons. To my children Gabriel and Corbin, I thank you for inspiring and teaching me to be a better person every day. To my siblings Anthony, Christian, Carolyn, and Robbie, your encouragement has meant the world to me. To all of my friends who have given me insight on life, suggestions, and brutal honesty, without you, life simply wouldn't be all that amazing. It has been a true gift to be a part of each of your lives. Without the experience, love, and presence, this book would not have been possible. This book has been independently written, edited and published in between a full-time job and mom duties. It is a combination of my heart, soul, fears, and doubts. Without a thought there is no dream. Without the dream, there is no drive for completion. As I leave a little piece of myself behind in this world, I hope that my dream helps you to see yours.

LC Owen is a native Texan and mother of two boys. When she is not writing or narrating for her podcast LC Owen Books, she enjoys singing karaoke with friends, going to local museums, or walking Reba (her dog). She released her first novel, The Islands of Sedania, in 2018. This is a three-part series in the romantic sci- fi/ fantasy genre that you don't want to miss. Please SUBSCRIBE to the LC Owen Books newsletter for free eBooks, eBook deals, and exclusive audios. LC Owen Books...Where thoughts become worlds!

Please #Follow

Instagram Facebook Twitter

CHAPTER 1

HE WANTS ME BACK

Who are we really? Are flesh and bones? Are we a soul or a brain? Can consciousness exist outside of the body? Does life keep repeating itself over and over again, hiding in the mask of reincarnation? Had I been on a journey, near death, or both? The questions twisted through my mind as I lay there, counting the dots on the ceiling. My sweaty palms stuck together as I began wringing my hands.

I certainly question which reality I dwell in and whether or not my existence is significant. If it is significant, then who is really missing me while I'm gone? Is it those on earth or the ones who exist in an alternate universe? Is the existence on another plane a prison or a freedom? After my escape from the Islands of Sedania, I found I was more confused than ever. I had convinced myself that it was a delusion my head had created to help me cope with the trauma of the car accident. I looked down at the off-white card with gold lettering as I twisted it through my fingers. Pressing my lips together, I tried to hold in the screams of my insanity. I couldn't keep it, nor could I throw it away. My fingers wrapped around the handle to my top dresser drawer, allowing it slide open. I stuffed the card beneath my silken underwear and socks, then slammed it closed. *That will have to do for now.* I thought. I *had* to maintain logic. What other alternative did I have? I wanted to believe that things were back to normal after all.   This new normal had an uncomfortable tinge of hardship without my mother by my side. Knowing that she was still deep in a coma in a hospital bed, I felt powerless. I would go through the motions of my life though. The boys would go to school by day and we would frequent the hospital by night. If I could wake up, then so could she. With each day that passed, the reality of the situation was becoming more and more grim.

"What's this?" I asked as the gray-haired doctor shoved a tri-fold pamphlet at me.

"It's some literature I want you to read. These decisions are never easy," he said.

When to cease life support. It read. I looked down at the pamphlet, not giving it even a second of thought before crumpling it in my fist and throwing it in the closest garbage can.

"Fuck you. My mom is going to wake up," I said.

I felt the need to justify keeping her alive. I knew in my heart I could win her back over to life. Every time I loomed over her bed, begging her to fight, her heart rate would increase just a bit as if to whisper that she heard me. It had been a week since my stay in the hospital and yet I tried to hold as still as possible, resisting any slight inclination of change. I couldn't roll with the change. I had to take small, baby steps each day to find my footing once again.

"Bye mom," said the boys as they wrapped their arms around my waist.

"Bye boys. Love you," I said.

"Love you too," they beamed.

Their little backpacks bounced as they stepped onto the morning school bus. I could see their big, doll eyes peering at me through the windows as they waved. My stomach wrenched with the uncomfortable pain of anxiety. *What if they don't come back this time?* I thought. It was a fear I would surely get over in time. The burden wouldn't just loom over me forever. Would it? I had a small bowl of chocolate ice cream by the cash register at work. There was a stack of boxes piled by the sales counter that needed to be put away. I sighed the heavy sigh of grief as I heaved them up into my arms and carried them to the back shelves. As I came back around the corner to the sales counter the ice-cream was beckoning me. I wrapped my fingers around the small spoon, allowing the frozen liquid to melt in my mouth. *Ding dong*, went the door. I looked up to see a tall gentleman in a long black coat appearing before me. His hair was jet black and eyes were sunken into his head. He was giving me a sharp expression, creating thick tension in the air between us.

"Can I help you?" I asked.

"Yes, do you have any causal shoes for men?" he asked. My heart thudded in my chest. I couldn't help, but feel the anticipation building.

"Of course, what size do you wear?"

"Twelve," he blurted.

"Okay, I'll be right back," I responded as I shuffled to the back room where the shelves were. I could see him seating himself on one of the stools. He crossed his legs and rested his hands on top of knees. His posture was proper, yet intimidating. I came out of the back room. Several shoe boxes were stacked up in my arms. I sat them next to him as I seated myself in the stool in front of him.

"Are you Ms. Liza Ward?" he asked. His tone was brash.

"Yes," I said looking up at him, preparing the shoe for his foot.

"Well, Ms. Ward, You've been served," he said in a matter of fact tone, handing me a manilla folder with a stack of papers. He got up and left, never trying any of the shoes on. Frazzled, I set the legal papers down on the counter of the store, putting each of the shoes away once again. *What just happened?* I thought.

My mother had apparently been summoned to court to determine fault in the accident. The man in the green truck had asserted fault against my mother, and because I was acting on her behalf the documents had made their way to me. I couldn't be bothered with legalities while my mother was fighting for her life. Who did this guy think he was anyway? He had some nerve being so damn proactive. I slumped down in the chair behind the sales counter, defeated by the circumstances.

I was no longer entrenched in the sorrow of the push-and-pull of romantic relationships, but instead a real and true sadness that was legitimately depressing. No longer was I in a nightmare that I could simply wake-up from, but I was faced with real life situations that could carry the heaviness of consequences. It made my previous life look like a cake walk in comparison. I knew I couldn't afford to take anything else for granted. I held the legal papers in my hands shaking at the thought. I would fight though. I *had* to. I had fought to get home and my fight wasn't over. Perhaps the cliché rang true: *That which didn't kill me made me stronger.* I certainly felt more empowered these days having declined Gary's offer to truly love me and all. What was one day in court anyway?

My phone dinged over an over again with sentiments from Gary, extending the pleasantries of his tongue. I felt the texts only provoked my indifference at this given moment. He was lamenting in the torture of no longer having me within his clutches. His chasing became aggressive and relentless. If only I had known before, that in my resistance I regained the power over him, I would have done it much sooner. The thing is, I probably did know, but I didn't have the emotional strength to find contentment in solitude. In my despair I had always reached out to him, trying to find momentary comfort in our physical connection without forcing him to see me in an emotional way. Now that he was on the receiving end of the chill of rejection, he couldn't stand it. Finally, I had regained my footing and stopped caring about conforming to the ideas of someone else's happiness. It's funny that way; men always wanting what they can't have. I didn't want to be someone's game. Not anymore. I just wanted to be loved, but the hope of that was even pushed far from my mind. I had my kids back. That's all I needed. Even if the whole experience was just a pure concoction in my mind, it made me look deep within myself and realize what was really important.

Holding the phone in my hand the illuminated screen bearing Gary's name was screaming at me to respond to his attempts at regaining my trust. I looked at the big gray bubbles of messages that he sent to me, clutching the phone in my palm, paralyzed. I wasn't paralyzed in the same manner I was before, hoping against hope that he would just message me, but rather still in my reaction to him. I no longer had the desire to answer him because his attention meant nothing anymore. He was a small speck in the past that didn't belong in my present or future. So, I put the phone back down in my purse, ignoring his every attempt to be back in my life. I shuffled back into the back room, putting away boxes of shoes and organizing the shelves when I heard the front door ding once again.

I rolled my eyes, letting out a heavy sigh at the thought of another mysterious man in a black coat who was there just to serve me. My hesitant feet walked out into the store. I peeked around the corner, as not to be seen by whomever might be lurking there. I could see the back of a bald man's head. The man was picking up the shoes, looking at them, and putting them back down again. It was Gary no doubt and I wasn't sure how I could face him. He turned around and I moved out of his sight, slinking back in the back room again.

"Liza, I know you're here. You might as well come out," he said. I was busted. I stepped out of the back room, looking him dead in his blue eyes.

"Gary, unless you're here to buy a pair of shoes, I suggest you leave," I said.

"Listen Liza, I know you said you never wanted to see me again, but please give me another chance. I think I've proven that I have real feelings for you. I want you back. Please don't do this," he pleaded.

"I don't think it's going to work out Gary," I said, looking down pretending to be busy with some paperwork. He placed his hands on top of mine.

"Liza, stop. Before the car accident you'd do anything to be with me. What happened?" he asked.

"My mother is in the hospital fighting for her life. I thought I lost my children. I've been too focused on you and all you do is take me for granted. I won't allow that anymore," I said. My voice was low and shaken.

"I know you're right baby. You're always right," he said putting his hands around my waist, pulling me in close to him.

I pushed back against him, turning to walk away and pretending to be busy positioning the items in the store. He again followed me, trying to stop me from what I was doing.

"It's no use Gary. Please just leave me alone. Our relationship is over," I blurted.

His hands found their way around my waist from behind, pulling me close to him. His breath warmed my neck as he whispered into my ear.

"Liza, I love you baby please," his whisper was low and sexy, awakening my inner desire for human touch.

I could feel his erection growing in his pants as he pressed up against me. His breath was heavy and clouded with desire. I closed my eyes for a moment, feeling lost in his embrace. He brushed my hair off my shoulder, fully exposing my neck and administering warm kisses. I turned around to look at him, putting my hands on his shoulders as our eyes met. His eyes sparkled with a warm intensity. He was wearing me down. I pushed him away again. *I must escape his trance.* I thought.

"Gary, please leave. Please," I said.

"What is it Liza? Why are you acting like this? Do you have another man or something?" he asked.

The question itself made my belly flutter with nerves. I did. I loved men that didn't exist. What the hell was wrong with me? Who would even love a woman with three bastard children in a crappy apartment over a shoe store? Gary was likely the best option I had, but that didn't sway me toward loving him again. The memory of Blane and Stark haunted me like a spirit in an abandoned insane asylum. The idea that I loved my delusion more than my real life made me think that perhaps I needed real professional help. If there's too much overlap between fantasy and reality, I could be really and truly certifiable.

"No Gary, there's not someone else. That's ridiculous. You, however, have several someone elses. So let's not play that game," I responded.

"I'm shocked you think that I ever cheated on you. I never did," he said.

"Do you really expect me to believe that? You're still fucking your ex-wife for God's sake," I responded.

"What? Sweetheart, I think you must have hit your head a little too hard. I'm not sleeping with my ex-wife nor is there anyone else; just you. I've been worried sick over you," he said.

"Well Gary, that's not really my problem. Now, please leave or I'll call the cops on you. You're not welcome here anymore," I said, busying myself in the store once more.

"Well, that baby you're growing is just as much mine as it is yours. You're not going to be able to get rid of me that easily," he said.

"Take me to court then Gary. I don't care. How are you so sure it's yours anyway?" I asked. He cocked his head as he looked at me. To him the question must have been ridiculous. He knew I had been obsessed him in an unhealthy way.

"Don't fuck with me. I know that baby's mine. It's obvious I've been the only object of your affection and I will be back in your life. Maybe you just need some more time, but you will be mine again," he growled.

"Just leave Gary. Please, just go," I commanded as I gestured toward the front door.

"Okay, fine. I'll go. I probably deserve all of this from you, but just know that I don't give up that easily," he said. His feet stopped against the floor as he pushed the front door open. It banged as his hand made contact with it and slammed closed behind him.

This time I didn't carry the burden of a sinking feeling, but rather the serenity of relief. It was a quiet feeling that everything was in it's right place, playing out exactly as fate would have it. I wasn't meant for Gary nor was he meant for me. Despite our mass of genetics that had found their way to one another inside my belly, I did not feel bound to this man. I was baffled by his display of desperation. Why had he fixated himself on me after having been so eager to let me go? I questioned whether or not it was fear of losing me to death, or the fact that his other options had fallen through. Perhaps he had a moment of clarity, feeling as though he had to put on a show for others. He couldn't look like a jerk after all. What kind of a man leaves his girlfriend after she survives a near fatal car crash and still manages to stay pregnant with his child? I didn't trust Gary's intentions. He didn't deserve one ounce of my dedication. I was more certain of that than anything in a time when nothing at all made sense.

Away from the pressure of his persistence, I relaxed my clenched nerves just a bit as if to rest from the stress of it all. It was almost more than I could bear. Syble appeared from outside the store window, iced coffee in hand. I knew she had just completed her morning workout and she was on her way to cheer me up. Beaming through my door, her smiling face greeted me with comfort. I knew she wore it to please me, not because it was genuine. She carried around just as much grief as I did, wondering if mom would be pulled back over the edge to life. None the less, I appreciated her effort to pretend things were normal. She always had a way of making me believe things weren't as bad as they were. I suppose it is our perception of things that make our reality real or not. With that logic, I had no reason to believe that Sedania wasn't a real place that I had visited, but I pushed that thought to the back of my head almost as soon as it made its presence known. I had to stop entertaining such silliness. There was no Blane or Stark, only the empty space in my heart for a lover and companion that was never filled in the first place.

"Hello beautiful!" she exclaimed, plopping the coffee down on the sales counter and sliding it toward me like a talented bartender.

"Hey Syble. What's new?" I asked.

"Oh, nothing much. I jut got done with my workout and thought you could use a little pick-me-up," she responded.

"You always know what I need. You're the best," I said, frowning.

"What's wrong Liza? I know your mom is still in the hospital, but you need to keep a positive outlook on things. Everything is going to be okay," she said.

"It's not that Syble. I mean, it is, but I have other things on my mind as well. If I told you, you'd think I was crazy," I responded. She looked at me, only raising a single eyebrow.

"Come on now. Do you really think that? I'm your best friend. You can tell me anything," she said.

"Well, while I was in the coma, some things happened that I can't explain, but I'm starting to think they were real," I started.

"Okay...." she said with skepticism.

"I fell in love with a man and then there was this other man and the children were lost on a forbidden island," I continued.

"You were just dreaming sweetie. It wasn't real. We came to visit you in your hospital bed. You were in a coma," she reasoned.

"I know. I told you it was crazy, but I received something in the hospital. I saved it. It's in the top drawer of my dresser. It's a card."

"You received a lot of cards while you were in the coma. There are a lot of people who just want you to be okay honey," she said.

"You don't understand. He sent me cards to direct me to the portal before. He's letting me know he's real. I can't get it out of my mind. I keep trying to convince myself it was all just a dream, but how could he have sent me the card? I have a longing in my heart for him and for another man too. It's hard to explain, but I can't ignore this. I don't even want Gary anymore," I said.

"That's because Gary is a jerk. This is nonsense, Liza. Just snap out of it. You're alive and well, ready to take care of your kids, that's all you need right now," she said trying to reason with me.

"I knew you wouldn't understand. Nobody will," I began to cry.

"Please don't do that honey. This whole thing has been really traumatic on you. I know a great psychiatrist who can help you out. My brother totally did a 180 after meeting this guy. I'll give you his number," she said, pulling out her cell phone to search for it.

"No Syble, I don't need a psychiatrist. I'm being serious. Why don't you believe me?" I asked.

"I do believe you honey. I believe you think it was real, but you have some things to face now and these illusions in your head are just going to cloud over your judgment. Just go once for me okay?" she said placing her hand on my shoulder.

"I'd do anything for you after what you did for me, but I'm not crazy am I?" I asked.

"No, you're definitely not crazy. I think you just needed a way to get over Gary and your brain created a way to cope with that. It's no big deal, but you may need a little professional help to get you over the hump, that's all," she said.

"Well, okay," I sighed. "I suppose you're right. I hope you're right."

"Of course I'm right Liza. I'm always right. Remember?" she asked. I smiled.

"Yes, I remember," I answered in a low voice.

"Now that's a good girl. Listen sweetheart, I gotta run, but go ahead and give this guy a call," she said jotting his phone number down and leaving it there on the sales counter next to my legal papers. I hugged her as she left, looking down at the phone number of the psychiatrist. Perhaps I was indeed crazy. If I was crazy though, I didn't want to be sane. I had to believe, even if only with a small piece of myself, that the experience I had was not in vain. How could I love people that weren't real to begin with? Why did I miss them? Why did I find myself wanting to go back to them? I had to find out if Sedania was a real place and I wasn't ready to accept that it had all been a fabrication.

CHAPTER 2

I'M NOT CRAZY

I clutched the off-white card in my hand as I sat and awaited my name to be called. I had decided to give this psychiatry thing a shot. My palms were sweating. I was shifting in my seat as the tight grip of anxiety clenched my insides. I knew I had to face my demons, but the admission of mental instability was a tough pill to swallow. I certainly didn't feel that I was crazy, but even Syble, who thought my craziest of my ramblings were normal, thought my proclamations were unsubstantiated. I know a car accident of this magnitude was no doubt cause enough for such delusions, but a part of me couldn't let it go. I had received another card. Blane knew how to lure me in. He had sent me several before. This was a tangible object in the real world I was experiencing. How could I ignore that?

As I sat in the waiting room, trying to busy myself with latest issue of Cosmopolitan, an old lady stepped out from the door that led to the doctors office, staring at me with intensity. Her harsh eyes conveyed a commanding tone. She resembled the old lady that I had seen at the red brick house with her messy waves of silver hair cascading over her shoulders and gnarly hands. As she stared at me she approached me in slow and steady way. I could feel an air of dominance as she came near to me. My heart was beating out of my chest. Her words would stay with me like train wreck. It was a mess I should flee from, but couldn't because of the magnitude of its impact.   "He doesn't give up. You drank from his cup. You can believe you're crazy and cry in it, but you made your bed, now lie in it," she said to me.

Her eyes were wide open on her stone cold and wrinkled face. My heart raced, paralyzed by her words. I held still like a statue, blinking in disbelief. I had to escape her, but how? I scrunched my eyes shut until every wrinkle on my face stood out. *This can't be real.* I thought to myself. When they opened again, the old woman had disappeared. Sweet relief came over me as I released my tensed muscles. I was thankful for her departure, yet she stood for something. It was confirmation that maybe I hadn't been dreaming after all. My body jolted forward as I marched over to the reception desk in the waiting room.

"Mam? Did you see that old woman? Where did she go?" I asked with a trembling voice.

"What old woman?" she responded.

"The one that was just standing right there! She spoke to me. Did you see her?" I exclaimed.

"Liza, you're going to have to sit down now. Dr. Samuels will be with you shortly," she said looking at me with the side-eye of disbelief.

I cowered down from my assertion, believing that my hallucinations had carried over from the head injury. *Of course she hadn't been there. She was just a figment of my imagination.* I thought. This further confirmed my need for psychiatric help. I buried my face again beneath the pages of Cosmopolitan, trying to show any sense of normalcy I could muster after my recent display. It was all I could do to pretend that lunacy had not overtaken me. I couldn't afford to be committed or treated like an outsider. I had a pressing court date to attend to after all. I wouldn't allow that man in the green truck to get away with what he had done to us, not after everything.

"Liza," called the lady behind the counter. I jumped. The magazine went flying into the air.

"Yes?" I responded.

"Dr. Samuels will see you now," she stated.

"Okay," I said as I stood.

I passed through the door that led me back to his office. It was the first door to the right as I entered the hallway. I sat down on the couch, awaiting his arrival. He had so many delicate things on his shelf. There was a picture of him with a much younger looking woman in an expensive silver frame. Next to it, was a glass ball that was suspended by a metal display. I could see every color of the rainbow as I peered inside of it. Next to the tan couch, was a box of tissues. There was a sign on the wall with a picture of the Cheshire cat that read 'We're all mad around here.' *Great.* I thought to myself. *He expects me to be a lunatic.* A short, balding man entered the room wearing wide rimmed glasses and carrying a clipboard. He sat down in his big easy chair looking at me and extending his hand to greet me.

"I suppose you're Liza," he said.

"Yes, I suppose so," I said shaking his hand.

"The pleasure is all mine. Now, what brings you here to me today?" he inquired.

He sat down and crossed his leg over his knee. He squinted as he looked down at the clipboard through his frames. His pudgy body leaned in. He tilted his head and angled his ear in my direction.

"Well, do I need to lay down on the couch or sit or what?" I asked.

I shifted in my seat, clasping my hands together. I began to fidget my thumbs as he looked back at me. I could feel the tense cord of nerves twisting inside of me.

"However you're most comfortable," he responded.

I laid down for a moment, but feeling a bit silly I sat up

again.

"Don't be nervous Liza. Let's just start from the beginning okay? What brings you here?"

"Well, I was in a car accident and hit my head. I went into a coma for four days," I began.

"Mmmhmm," he affirmed, looking down at his clipboard. The motion of his pen as he scribbled across his paper reminded me of a horse race. He must have been hanging on my every word.

"The thing is, I don't remember being in the accident. Well, I do, but the way I remember it, we missed the green truck and went on our way," I said.

"Well, the brain is a funny thing. Sometimes we can't recall the details of traumatic accidents because our brains cancel out the trauma and replace it with something else. That doesn't sound out of the ordinary to me," he said. He shrugged, resuming his scribble on the paper. He crinkled his eyebrows as his hands formed the letters.

"I appreciate that, but there's more," I said. I shifted in my seat again. I could feel my palms turning clammy with anxiety.

"My children disappeared into an alternate universe and in order to get them back I had to go with a man called Blane through the portal. He took both my mother and me. He loved me though and he tried to convince me to stay on his island in paradise. The only reason I said no was because I had to get my kids back. They were with Blane's mother Issiryth you see. She took them to her island" I stopped. He only nodded his head and continued on with his pen.

"Are you getting all this?" I asked.

"Yes, please continue," he said.

"Well, there was a man there called Stark who helped me escape. I got to Issiryth's island to get them. I loved Stark too, but he died and I had to face Issiryth alone. Then, when I got them back, I woke up and they told me I had been in a coma," I said.

"Why did you have to escape Blane if he loved you and you wanted to stay with him? Was he holding you captive?" he asked.

"Well, no...Kind of. I don't know. He just wanted me to stay there with him and I couldn't. So, Stark helped me to turn into a mermaid so I could swim to Issiryth."

"Why couldn't you just take a boat over to her?"

"Because if I did that, I would get killed by a mermaid or an ulmiliac," I said.

"What is an ulmiliac?"

"It's a sea monster," I replied.

"How did you meet Stark? What's the story on him?" he asked.

I let out a sigh of frustration. *Did I really need to explain this again?*

"I tried to steal his boat to get across to Issiryth, but he saved my life," I said.

"You nearly lost your life?" he asked.

"Oh, never mind. This was such a bad idea. I know I'm crazy okay? But this all felt real to me. Trying to explain it all to you now makes me see how ridiculous all of this really is," I said.

I gathered my purse in my hand as I allowed the strap to rest over my shoulder. I stood up to leave, but as I did so, he frowned.

"Liza please, have a seat," he said motioning for me to sit down. "I want to hear the rest."

"You think all of this is bullshit don't you?" I asked.

"It sounds like the experiences you had were real to you. I'm not going to downplay that. Like I said, the mind is a funny thing. Sounds like you had a traumatic experience," he advised.

"So, there's no way it really happened right?" I asked.

"Not if you were in a coma," he said.

"Well, I saw an old lady in the waiting room. She said something about me drinking from a cup and lying in the bed I made. Was that a hallucination?" I asked.

"I see Mrs. Timball every week," he responded.

"Well the receptionist said she didn't see her. The old lady said some things to me that were very familiar and I've seen her before. I saw her in the red brick house after my kids disappeared and she said some pretty creepy things back then also."

"Okay, what did she say?" he asked.

"I don't want to talk about it, but something else happened. I got this card in the hospital," I said. I unzipped my purse and clutched the card in my fingers. I extended it out in front of me and began to wave it in his face.

"It's off-white with gold lettering."

"Okay. I see that. What significance does that have?" he asked.

"Blane always sent me these cards with the gold lettering when he wanted to tell me something. I got this and it's from Blane!" I exclaimed.

"Okay, what does the card say?" he asked.

"It says: I hope you're happy now."

"Okay, well it's just a card Liza. How do you know it was intended for you?" he asked.

"It was addressed to me! If he were a fabrication of my mind, how would he have sent me a physical card?" I asked.

"Liza, I don't know where that card came from, but I assume there's a perfectly logical explanation for all of this and the answer isn't that you were in an alternate universe. Let's look at your kids for example. They were alive and well the entire time correct?" he asked.

"Yes," I responded.

"You've been through a lot, but that doesn't mean you're crazy. I'm going to prescribe you some medication to help out with your anxiety, but I think you just need to take it easy and move on with your life as you normally would. I'll see you next week," he said.

"That's it? You're just going to medicate me and send me on my way?" I asked.

"Well, what else would you have me do?"

"I don't know. Comfort me? Tell me I'm going to be okay?"

"Liza," he paused. "You're going to be okay."

"Okay," I said. I snatched the paper prescription from his hand. My heart sank as I moved my feet across the floor with the heaviness of disappointment.

As I walked to the reception desk to pay for my visit, I could hear Dr. Samuels speaking into a recorder in his office. He was making audio notes of our visit.

"Patient suffered traumatic brain injury, claiming delusions to be authentic," he said.

He was substantiating my madness. I could feel the heat of anger welling up to my flushed face. *What sort of professional did such a thing?* I thought. I could hear the sound of my ringing phone, muffled by the material of my purse. I swished my hand around inside. Finally locating it, I held it in my hand and peered into the illuminated screen.

"Gary again," I scoffed.

I pressed the 'send to voicemail' button. *Why didn't he get it? I was done.* The voice mail alert dinged right away. *I should just ignore it. Right?* The subtle feeling of paranoia and curiosity began to creep up inside of me though. What if it was important? What if he needed to tell me something I hadn't considered? What if he was stalking me and I needed to report it to the police? With an impulsive finger and manic mind, I pressed the voicemail button and put the receiver up to my ear. It was muffled and the bass of the man's voice didn't match that of Gary's. It was a different, yet familiar. As it cut in and out, I was only able to make out a few clear words. Liza... I miss you...Come back to me...I forgive you... If you come, I'll give her back.

All of it sounded similar to the things Gary had been telling me over the last few days. All with the exception of 'If you come, I'll give her back'. What on earth could that mean? It didn't even make sense for Gary to say such a thing. The voice itself didn't even sound like him. Who could it be then? Blane? I had to dismiss that. It was insane. My finger pressed the delete button, erasing any evidence I could refer back to that would keep my delusion alive. I had hoped this mental illness would be short lived, releasing me from the clutches of pretend so that I could return the normalcy of my real life.

My car tires screeched in the parking lot as I pressed my foot into the gas pedal. I couldn't shake off the feeling of anger. These small coincidences all seemed to add up to something. Something strange and sinister. Something I knew I had to let go of, yet it wouldn't let go of me.

"Damn you!" I yelled shaking my fist.

I turned the corners with a sharp turn of my steering wheel. The tires of my car screamed as they skidded on the road. It almost felt as if it was tilting sideways each time I rounded a corner. It would be safe to assume after the car accident I was in, I would be less inclined to drive in such a manner. I was insane though. I must have been and I didn't care. I approached the small downtown area of the city where my shoe store sat tucked on a quiet street corner. There was an intersection just in front of it. As the light turned yellow, my foot was like a heavy brick on the pedal. Just as I had made the decision to go for it, I could see a person was trying to cross the street. In a split second decision, I slammed on the brakes, skidding my car tires down the road. My car came to a screeching halt within in inches of a human being. The lady stopped in her tracks holding still and looking straight at me with her sharp, icy blue eyes. It was the old lady I had seen in the waiting room and at the red brick house. She wouldn't move or do anything other than stare right through me. My heart leaped out of my chest, just staring back at her. My breath fell heavy and furious. I could feel the soreness in my lungs as I let the air in and out of them. I doubled over in hyperventilation. *This isn't happening. This isn't happening.* I thought. Her eyes were angry looking through me as if I had ruined her perfect day. She mouthed something to me through the window, but I couldn't make out her words. My face scrunched up as I held my eyes shut.

"This isn't real. It isn't real," I said out loud.

I jumped at the sound of a horn honking behind me. I threw up my hands in defiance.

"Can't you see there's a lady trying to cross the street?!" I rebutted.

I turned back around to look. There was no lady crossing the street. She was gone and my light was as green as the grass on a spring day. Embarrassed at my outward display of inadequacy, I pushed on the gas with my head down. I gave the gas a slow push of my foot as I rolled into the back parking space below my apartment. I would have to let this go and I knew that. None of this was real. I had a real life I had to face and I knew it. I was thankful that in my experience, I had found the strength to resist Gary, but I had taken on a whole other heap of burdens. Perhaps the throws of insanity weren't the worst possible fate after all. In the craziness, I found myself comforted by the hope that there may be something lurking for us on the other side beyond this life that we know. I hadn't been inclined to step beyond the boundaries of my comfort in the past, but now all I wanted was to be validated in the realness of what had happened to me. I had loved and lost time and time again, but nothing compared to knowing that Blane and I were separated by reality and fiction. Stark and I had been separated by life and death. I loved them both in different ways, yet I didn't even know if they were real at all.

CHAPTER 3

THE PORTAL AWAITS

Despite my best effort to convey stability, it seemed like things would keep cropping up in my life. I was constantly confronted by the islands. I didn't know how much more I could take without feeling swayed over by my fantasy. So, I stayed there in my apartment waiting for the boys to get home from school and hoping that I would be able to forget what had happened. I sat down on the couch, flipping through the channels on the TV, not really watching nor listening. This aimless venture was a mere distraction as I was drumming my fingers on the arm of the sofa, craving my chocolate ice cream. The pit of my stomach felt like a twisted mess of anxiety. Unable to distract myself, I knew the sweetness of the frozen treat would be the only remedy. Rising from my place in the couch, I walked upon my freezer, revealing the ice cream I had allowed to melt on my bedside table the night before the car crash. I pried open the lid and dug a large scoop of the refrozen goop out and into my bowl as I shuffled back away to my place in the living room. I plopped down with my ice cream, shoveling it in my mouth like a zombie. With each bite I took, the large chunks of frozen chocolate would melt away on my tongue, turning into a fountain of chocolate cascading down into my eager belly.   I blinked, trying to fool myself into believing that I was actually occupied with the pictures on the screen, but that couldn't have been further from the truth. I was locked in my neurosis. My mind's eye was busied with visions of the island. My fingers moved through the golden sand along the beach, feeling the warmth of the sun kissing my skin. I could see Blane's adoring eyes looking down at me as I lied there in the sand, soaking in the leisure of our paradise. We could admire the beauty in one another without the utterance of one single word. With only a touch and a gaze, I knew he was mine. Yet, within the tranquility of this daydream, my mind still raced with the memory of Stark who so bravely fought the ulmiliac if only to help me reach safe passage to Issiryth's island. *It had to be real.* I thought to myself, shoving more of the refrozen chocolate goop into my mouth and watching the pictures on the TV dance about. Behind my eyes, inside this mind of mine, I had a memory of a love lost; a love I wanted to get back more than anything.

I scooped the last bit of ice cream in my mouth, allowing the bowl and spoon to fall into the couch as I layed my head back and closed my eyes. Only a few small tears managed to escape.

"Blane," I whispered out into the universe, hoping my message would be carried all the way to Sedania and reach his ears.

No sooner did his name escape my lips, did the floor vibrate beneath me, causing the lamp on the table to tumble over and crack. I jumped up off the couch, startled by the commotion. I bounded away to the kitchen for a broom and dust pan. As I scooped up the broken glass, I was startled by yet another noise. The front door rattled and shook. I was paralyzed. I could feel the adrenaline shooting through my extremities. My sweaty palm wrapped around the handle of the broom as I held it up in the air. As I prepared to strike, two tiny faces bounced through the front door.

"Mommy are you okay?" asked Noah.

"Yea mom. What are you doing?" asked Jameson.

I threw the broom to the side and pulled my arms in close to my to my body. I shook my head as I looked down at the ground.

"I'm sorry guys. The lamp broke. I was just cleaning it up," I said.

"Okay, I'm hungry," whined Noah.

"Me too," Jameson agreed.

"Okay then, guys. Go get something to eat out of the pantry. You know where the snacks are, then get your homework out asap," I responded.

"Yes mam," they said in unison making their way back to the kitchen.

I could hear the crinkling of wrappers, the thud of plastic cups slamming down on the counter, and liquid pouring out and splashing into the bottom of them. The sounds of their little voices, trying to overpower each other, echoed throughout my house like a booming voice in a cavern. The zippers of their backpacks zinged open as their books and folders smashed onto the kitchen table. To any mother these would be familiar sounds, but to me it was reassurance that I had my boys safe and sound. I would relish these moments when I could hear the sound of them going about their after school activities. My heart fluttered in contentment as I picked up the remainder of the pieces of the lamp off the floor and marched them over to the waste receptacle.

"Mom, will you help me with my homework?" Noah asked.

"What is it?"

"It's math homework," he responded.

"Can you have your brother help you sweetheart? Mommy needs to make a phone call," I said.

"No, I want you to help me," he said.

"Okay baby, just give me one second," I responded, moving into my bedroom.

I shut my bedroom door, allowing my back to press up against it. My finger hit the dial button on my phone. I had to call Syble. I wanted to tell her about every strange experience that I had just had, but I was still faced with her potential disbelief. *Who else would I tell though?*

"Hey beautiful," she answered.

"Hey Syble, how's it going?" I asked.

"It's going. How was Dr. Samuels?" she asked.

"Oh, he's alright I guess, but I didn't care for him," I responded.

"Why Liza? What happened?" she asked.

"Nothing happened really. He just said I'm fine and prescribed me a medication for my anxiety," I responded.

"Okay? Isn't that what he's supposed to do?"

"Yes, I suppose, but I heard him talking on his voice recorder thing about me."

"What did he say?"

"He said I think my delusions are authentic."

"Well, do you think that Liza?"

"No....Yes...I don't know," I said putting my head down. "Some things have happened today Syble. How do I explain the card in the hospital or the old lady in the waiting room?"

"Slow down Liza. What old lady are you talking about?"

"The old lady I saw in the red brick house when I dropped the boys off. You know when they disappeared?" I said growing frustrated.

"The boys didn't disappear. That's crazy okay? This is reality. This is what really happened! They were with Wendy and when she couldn't get ahold of you, she called the local hospital. When the hospital located you and your mother, they tried to contact Jace, but he's living in Arizona or something. He told them to get ahold of me because I'm your best friend. So, the hospital gave Wendy my phone number and I came to get them. They stayed at my house for four days while you were in a coma and we visited you every night. I told them you were just resting and you'd wake up. That's what happened, okay? That's it. There was no portal, or old lady, or disappearance. The kids were safe the whole time."

Her tone was sharp and confrontational. It was not the soothing voice I could normally expect. *Why didn't she just be-*

lieve me?

"Then why do I feel Blane all the way down to my bones? Why do I miss him? Why do I cry for Stark, the man who died for me? Why do I miss the way Leila laughed with me as she helped me get dressed and fix my hair? How can I have real feelings for people and relationships that aren't real? Can you tell me that? How?" I yelled. I was just trying to make sense of it all.

"I don't know, but you have to snap out of this. Whatever you experienced didn't happen because obviously the kids were safe the whole time and we saw you laying there sleeping in a coma. I've been through a lot thinking I had lost you and trying to take care of the boys. I've been waiting and wondering if I would be responsible for them or if they'd go live with their dad who's practically a stranger. I've always been there for you. I've wiped away your tears and talked to you for hours while you sobbed over Gary, but I can't comfort you over your delusions. It's beyond my area of expertise or understanding. I'm sorry. Whatever you think you saw or experienced, just push it to the back of your mind because it's not real okay? It's just not!" she pleaded.

I felt tears welling up inside of me. I knew I was truly alone in this. I was away from the comfort of my mother and my best friend. Nobody would understand. I would have to simply stop talking about or entertaining it.

"Okay Syble, you're right. I'll stop talking about it now. It's done, okay," I said.

My finger pressed against the disconnect button. I had nothing further to discuss with her. My phone began to ring, buzz, and ding as I buried it in my purse. I wasn't going to call her back. I wasn't going to speak to her at all. She didn't understand. I fell face-first into a sea of pillows lined up on my bed. I laid face down in them, screaming as loud as my lungs would allow. Inside the cushion of the pillow, I was muffled. I wasn't just sad. I could feel the ugliness of anger setting in. I began to toss the pillows and destroy the flatness of the bed clothes by rumpling them up and pulling them away from the mattress. My beet red face turned splotchy with the rush of tears as my feet stomped into the floor beneath me.

"Blane, I know you're there! I know you're watching me! Why don't you just come out and face me?" I yelled, holding my arms out to each side. "Blane, come back and show yourself!"

I could hear my ceiling fan overhead, buzzing as the pull chains clanked against the light fixture. I scanned the room for any small, simple sign that he may be lurking about, but still there was nothing, only the sound of the fan. I held very still, only moving my eyes to check for any signs of him. From the corner of my eye, I could see a flickering light taunting me with its mystery. As I turned to look at it, my bedside table lamp was switching itself on and off.

"Blane, is that you?" I asked speaking out into the air. "Where are you?"

The light bulb faded in and out like a strobe light. *Was this his confirmation message?* I could see the lampshade rotating around. An old glass of water I had left there beside it, was rippling with vibration. Like an oncoming storm, I could feel the activity in my room beginning to kick up at my request for Blane's presence.

"Come on Blane. I know that's you! Just come out if that's what you're going to do," I said.

The floor beneath me shook like an earthquake. I put my hands out for stabilization, but I was unable to stay in a standing position. I tumbled down to the ground like timbered tree. I tried to remain calm, but I found it difficult. The floor beneath me continued to tremble with the reminder of my delusion. Soon the sounds of rushing water could be heard coming from closet. My feet labored to stay planted on the floor. With each step I took, the ground shook beneath me. My arms extended to each side trying to maintain balance. As I opened the double doors leading to my closet, a gusting breeze threw my hair over my shoulders. I was standing on the edge of a rocky cliff, leading all the way down to a cascading waterfall.

"Jump Liza," I heard a voice say to me.

I gave each handle of my closet door a firm grasp. I knew this waterfall all too well. The consequences of jumping may put me in a position I wasn't ready to be in again. Blane would have to find his way to me, not the other way around. I would never leave my precious children again of that I was certain. With each of my arms, I held strong in the midst of the chaos, with the moving ground beneath my feet. My face scrunched up as I closed my eyes.

"No, not this way! I wont leave them again!" I yelled out.

My arms strained as I pulled each side of my closet door closer, and closer together. My eyes were still shut. *This isn't real. My inner voice yelled at me. This is just a dream. Wake up.* Pulling with all my might, I managed to get the doors almost shut. As they touched one another, I was thrown back up into the air and fell flat on my back. The room stopped shaking all at once and I was able to stand up again. I ran over to my closet doors and opened them only to reveal a rack full of clothes. Relieved, I ran out my bedroom door to check on the boys who were still doing homework and slamming apple juice at the kitchen table.

"Are you okay guys?" I asked. They looked at me with puzzled faces.

"Yes," said Jameson.

"Did you feel that shaking? There must have been an earthquake or something," I said.

"No, we didn't feel anything," Noah said.

"Ya'll didn't feel anything?" I asked. Their innocent eyes looked up at me as they shook their heads. *The whole damn floor had shaken. How in the hell had they not felt anything?* I thought to myself.

"Okay, Mommy isn't feeling well. I'm going to go lie down for little bit. Are y'all good?"

"Yea we're good Mom. We're almost done. Can we play video games now?" Jameson asked.

"Of course guys whatever you want," I said.

My legs were feeble like a newborn lamb. I was mindful not to shut my door this time. *Perhaps if I left it open, nothing strange would happen.* I thought. Collapsing on my bed, I melted away in the covers like butter on a hot baked potato. I was infused with the comfort of my own scent. I was home now and that alone was something I couldn't afford to take for granted. Having seen the waterfall again with my own eyes made it entirely plausible that I would get drawn back into the fantasy. I was like an moth to a light bulb. I just couldn't stay away. It was hard enough to be entirely in love with a man who didn't exist by any stretch of the imagination and mourning another who was equally as fictional. How would I find myself out of the maze of mystery? I would have to turn the corners carefully, eliminate the dead end pathways, and feel my way to the end . Would willpower alone be enough to rid me of my affliction? I feared not, but despite that, I had to try.

The boys could be heard in the next room playing their video games and shouting over one another. A recent annoyance was now music to my ears. I listened with great pleasure, etching the memory of their voices into my eternal file folder. It's funny how every moment can be seen in either the light of positive or the murkiness of negative. The dark cast of small nuisances can brighten into shiny new experiences with the slightest tweaking of a twisted mind. The beautiful mess that was my scrambled brain may have been a blessing in disguise. The struggle shaped me and changed the way I thought about things. My dream may have been just that, but in having it, I found my strength.

Leaving Blane and losing Stark were no doubt some of the most devastating losses I had ever experienced. I was torn between two men, but fate tore me apart from them both. I wanted so badly to believe that I could get back to Blane. I wanted answers to my questions. Was my mom trapped there? I closed my eyes, imagining the last time I saw her. I remember the confusion in her eyes as I hugged her and called her mom. It's as if she remembered me even though her mind was telling her she didn't. With her life hanging in the balance, I knew I had bigger fish to fry. The struggle was just beginning and the dream was just a dream. It was not only a struggle of my logical mind versus the dream world, but a struggle to keep my mom alive and clear her name in this horrific car accident. I still had trouble believing it actually had happened in the first place, but I was left no other alternative.

I pulled the legal papers out from the drawer of my bedside table to read who I was up against. Who was this man accusing my mother of such a thing? He had to be out of his mind. I shuffled the papers out of the manila folder, revealing the name my most recent nemesis. Plaintiff: Virgil S. Finkleman, it read. His name sounded like a dorky old man who'd escaped from the old folks home in a stolen green truck. The name alone made me feel less threatened by his current presence in my life. He was now another nuisance, hovering over my life like a buzzing fly. I could easily swat it out of existence. I laughed to myself having read through the documents, making light of the situation. *Virgil Finkleman.* I thought. *Who would bestow such a horrid name on their child?* Delighted by the humor, I shoved it back down into the manila folder and back into the drawer of my bedside table. A smile passed by my lips as I laid there still listening to the ruckus of my children. I contemplated all the possibilities. *This is going to be a piece of cake.* I thought to myself.

CHAPTER 4

IZZY

"B..B...," Noah sputtered.

"Beauty," I responded.

"Beauty Buzzy was a bee. She lived in a hive in a tree. She made sweet honey all day long and played in the fl....fl.....," he read.

"Flowers," I said.

"Flowers singing her song," Noah labored over his favorite book.

They say reading to your loved ones while they're in a coma is supposed to help. Jameson played with his tablet. He was sitting on the stiff pleather couch beside her bed. I suppose he was just trying to tune out the tragedy.

"Very good honey. You read that like a champ!" I exclaimed. "You can put it away now. She really liked it."

"How can you tell?" he asked.

"I just can," I said. I turned to kiss her forehead. "I love you mom. We'll be back tomorrow. You have to fight okay? I'm going to win your court case tomorrow."

Her heart rate would increase at the sounds of our voices, almost as if she knew we were there. I knew she could wake up if she wanted to. I just hoped that she would. After several days, I had been incident free of Blane or his world, but that didn't stop me from believing that it might be real. I wanted to believe it wasn't. So, I put all my focus on mom, her court case, and bringing her back over to life. There was still that small shimmer inside of me that I couldn't shake though. On the way home, the boys and I bounced along to the songs on the radio, each taking our individual turns singing solos. Jameson would do his goofy face while rocking his head back and forth and Noah would pretend he had a microphone. It was as if the pep in the music would rev us up to face the tragedy that our lives were. These poor boys had been through so much. I can't imagine how their lives would have turned on their heads completely had I not awoken from the coma.

"Mom, can I have a computer?" Jameson asked.

"A computer? What do you need a computer for?" I asked.

"So, I can play games and stuff," he responded.

"Well, you play games on your console in the living room," I responded.

"Yea, but different games. Computer games," he said.

"No, I don't think you need a computer," I said.

"Awe! Why mom? That's not fair!" Jameson whined

"Yea," Noah chimed in. "That's not fair. Izzy would get us one if we wanted."

"Izzy?" I asked puzzled. "Who is Izzy?"

"Shhhh Noah. We aren't supposed to talk about her!" Jameson interjected.

"Her!?" I exclaimed. "Boys tell me what you're talking about right now."

"We can't mom. We promised her we wouldn't tell you. It's nothing bad," Jameson said.

"I need to know right now guys. You shouldn't be talking to strangers or people I don't know. That's just dangerous. You have to tell me. I'm your mom!" I exclaimed.

"She does know you mommy. She said she knows you," Noah said.

"Shut up Noah!" Jameson yelled, punching his brother in the arm. Noah began crying.

"Stop it guys! Stop it right now! I need to know what you guys are talking about it!" I yelled. I pulled over the car to the side of the road turning around to look them squarely in their little eyes in the back seat. "I'm not moving this car until you guys tell me what you're talking about!"

"See what you've done," Jameson said thumping Noah in his arm.

"Ow!" he screamed.

"Cut that out Jameson. There's no need for that!" I said. "Now, one last chance. Tell me what's going on."

The car grew quiet as neither one of them wanted to come clean. Jameson sighed.

"Izzy is just a lady. She visits us when we go to bed," he said.

"Oh my God! Does she touch you inappropriately? Did someone touch you while I was in the coma? Oh my God I'm going to kill her! Did Syble have friends over while you guys were staying over?" I began to panic

"No mom. It's not like that," Jameson said. "She's a lady, but Syble doesn't know her."

"I don't understand. A lady visited you in bed?" I asked puzzled.

"No, she visits *when* we go to bed," Jameson answered.

"Yea mom she does fun stuff with us and shows us cool things too," Noah said.

"Like what?" I asked.

"Like we get to ride horses on her beach or fly kites," Noah said.

"Her beach?" I gasped. "She has a beach?"

"Well yea she's on an island or something. She does fun stuff with us and then puts us back to bed. She told us not to tell you," Jameson said elbowing his brother. "It's like we go somewhere else."

"Somewhere else?" I said in a low voice, backing down from my mama bear attitude. It dawned on me who they were talking about, but it couldn't be. Could it?

"Issiryth..." I let out a small whisper.

"You do know her mommy!" said Noah.

"No, I don't," I rebutted.

"But you just said her name!" Noah argued.

"No, I didn't. Just stop guys. There is no Izzy. If she visits you again, you tell her you're not going with her. She's not real! Do you understand me?" I asked.

"But mom..." Jameson began.

"No, 'but mom'! There is no Izzy! Do you understand me?" I asked again.

"Yes mam," they said in unison.

"Good then," I smiled. "Let's get home!"

I pretended as if the conversation hadn't taken place, going back to the dancing and singing in the car as we drove home. I could tell the boys were uncomfortable with what they had just confessed. I didn't know if Issiryth was real or not, but the fact that I wasn't the only one spouting off about the islands made me feel a bit better. I pulled up to our apartment, opening the car doors for the boys to step out and escort me to the top of the stairs. We filed in as we always had.

"Okay boys. Time to get ready for bed. Ya'll are sleeping in my room tonight, okay?" I said.

"Yay!" Noah yelled, running into the bathroom for his nightly bath.

"Mom," Jameson started.

"Yes?" I answered.

"Why can't we talk about Izzy?" he asked.

"Because we don't talk about things that aren't real," I said.

"Why not? We talk about Santa Clause and he's not real," he said.

"Now that's not true Jameson! Why would you say that?"

"Because I saw you putting my bicycle out at Christmas. I wasn't asleep all the way," he responded.

"Now that's just not good! How do you know I wasn't just

rearranging it after Santa got here with it?" I asked. Jameson looked at me as if that were a very silly statement.

"Come on mom, I know that's not true. Why can't we talk about Izzy? She's real to us. Just as real as you and me," he said looking up at me. His eyes were so raw and innocent.

"Because, I can't entertain thoughts of a woman coming to visit and taking you and brother away from me," I responded.

"She doesn't take us away from you because she always gives us back. She said she saw you get hit by a green truck and thought we might be sad and worried so she came to visit us to cheer us up," he said.

"Well, that's very kind, but I think you and Noah are just dreaming when you see her and dreams aren't real. They're just how our minds cope with trauma. We replace the trauma with something else. It doesn't mean anything. Now, just forget her okay? She's not your reality. I'm your reality. I'm mom and I'm always here for you. Do you get me?" I asked holding his cheeks together and making him look at me.

"Yes, I get you mom. We wont talk about her anymore," he said.

"You promise?" I asked.

"Yes, I promise," he said.

"Let's pound on it," I said extending out my fist. He met my fist with his for fist bump and explode, then went off into his bedroom to get ready for bed.

I sat back in my living room chair thinking of the words the boys had said about how Issiryth had visited them. I wanted them close to me if only to ensure that she wouldn't take them again, but had she even taken them at all? I knew it was best if I told the boys not to speak of her. Not only because I was try-ing to convince myself she wasn't real, but because I didn't want them to fall into the same pit of insanity.

As I tucked the kids into my bed with me that night, I had hoped we would just sleep without the interruption of anything else. I curled up next to them, just placing my hands on their chests to feel them rise and fall with each breath. Noah's little fingers wrapped around mine, patting my hand as he did so. Their doll-like faces relaxed with each breath in their innocent expressions. In a peaceful slumber, we drifted away together, certain of the safety we found in one another. We were no doubt creating new memories, new dreams, and new experiences, but none of us dared to speak of them. If we did, it may make our reality less desirable. I knew I had to be strong for my day in court and the boys felt they had to be strong for me. Was it their burden? No, but we often take on burdens for the ones we love if only to sooth them in their angst. My boys were no exception. They were like beacons of hope in the despair of real life. Their very presence as we slept was enough to keep me content for one more night. So, there I stayed in that moment for a small shimmer of hope.

Little did I know that within the bliss of our dreams laid the opportunity to get reeled-in again. I could feel the boys tossing in their sleep, waking me each time they did so. I would rub my hand down their backs to calm them, telling them to just go back to sleep. I could assure them a dream was only a dream, but it was concept more loose in definition. I wasn't certain a dream was only a dream. It could be any number of things and I could no longer subscribe to an understanding of what it was. As lightly as I slept that night, with the distractions of each worry, my eyes would eventually always grow heavy again. My mind tormented me with the visions of Sedania. I could feel the heaviness of Blane's body on top of mine, reminiscent of the shadow who visited me the night before the car crash. His weight on my body , both a comfort and a fright, rendered me inanimate. I wanted to embrace him, but in the same accord, I needed him to leave me alone. The sensations of his touch caressed my body like the ocean waves on his sandy beach.

"You'll be home soon Liza," he whispered as his shadowy form dissipated into the abyss of the universe.

No longer could I feel the warmth of his skin, but was rather shaken awake for the fifth time by the restlessness of my thoughts. My boys tossed about in the bed again, showing signs of emotional discomfort.

"Shhhh, it's okay. Go back to sleep honey," I comforted each time, then fell away to my own dreams again. If I was going to see someone, I had hoped to see Stark once more, but his face never appeared in my visions. It was as if Blane were monopolizing the space in my brain, still conflicting me with whether or not I wanted to love him forever. It was unfair of him to task me with such a responsibility if he were indeed real.

"Blane, just leave me alone. I have to take care of mom," I said. I hoped he could hear me.

The floor shook beneath us, then at once stopped. My arms took a tight grasp on my boys. I knew it would be dangerous for my children to experience it, but luckily they did not awake from their sleep. I wondered if they had seen Issiryth that night or what promises she delivered to them. I knew I should not use his name. My lips retracted backward into tight silence. Armed with that assertion, I fell asleep once more, only awaking again to the sound of my alarm.

CHAPTER 5

A DAY IN COURT

I stood there in front of my mirror adjusting my clothes. The boys had just gone off to school. I had to look just right, after all. I was wearing a black pinstripe skirt that came just above the knee. I adjusted the matching blazer as I turned back and forth. My attorney's words were ringing through my head.

"Use your big brown eyes to look innocent," he said. "If they think you're sweet and trustworthy. They'll take your side."

I widened my eyes, then narrowed them again. I wasn't sure if I looked innocent enough. I looked like I knew what the hell I was talking about at least. That's all that was important My long brown hair fell over my shoulders as I brushed it. I really couldn't match the hair magic that Leila always had with me. As much as I tried to replicate it, her craft was unmatched. I so wished I could just put her in my pocket and take her away from Blane's island, but she made it apparent that she would never oblige me with her friendship again. It was another loss to add to the many I was currently experiencing. I drove away to my destination with a blank approach; trying to snuff out any emotion.   Pulling up to the courthouse that day, I said a small prayer to myself. It's not as if I even believed there was a God, but in this moment of desperation I felt that something or someone beyond my comprehension holding a higher power, must be looking down on me. I wondered what he may have thought of me or how he regarded my actions. Would I even be a candidate for help? Most likely not. I had only found cause to reach out in my lowest of moments, defeated by the hardship of life. My heels clicked on the cement as I climbed the stairs and opened the big doors to the courthouse. There stood my lawyer, with his short gray hair and a goatie. He was all dressed up in his Armani suit. I could see his thirsty eyes checking out my body from head to toe. Although he never acted on his urges, I could feel the energy of his arousal.

"You look great Liza," he said. "Are you okay? Do you remember the things we discussed?"

"Yes," I responded. "I think so."

"Good. Don't be nervous. Everything is going to be okay," he said, rubbing my shoulder.

"Yea, I know," I said nodding.

We walked into the courtroom and took our places on the defendant side. My attorney placed his hand in the small of my back as he scooted my body into the chair he had pulled out for me. Looking over at the empty chairs of the plaintiff side, I eagerly awaited laying my eyes on Mr. Finkleman. I wondered how his mannerisms would portray themselves to the jury. My attorney was fairly assured that my look alone was enough to sway them. My mother was in a coma and I was struggling as a single mom, after all. My situation rang true with many sisters, daughters, aunts, and cousins. The common American man or woman would understand and take pity on such a thing. Mr. Finkleman had already presented himself as a bully. I was told that although he had connections and wealth, I had sympathy on my side.

As I took several deep breaths, my attorney poured me a glass of water and whispered encouraging words of success in my ear. My throat tightened with the grip of anxiety, shooting through insides and churning the acid in my stomach. My palms, face down on the table, permeated with beads of sweat as my heart raced; pumping a million molecules of angst through my veins. I could feel the heaviness of a thousand questions from attorneys who are trained to twist my words like a road that wraps around the mountainside. As each scenario presented itself to my mind, I felt the squeeze of immense pressure. The chatter of spectators behind me, chewed away at my brain, bit-by-bit, like a bird pecking at the ground. I could hear the courtroom doors opening as two men in suits entered, announcing their presence without the utterance of a single word. It was in in their manner and demeanor that they commanded attention, scowling as they did.

The first man, holding a briefcase, was of average height with stark white, slicked back hair. He had a large birthmark on his forehead that stood out with the crinkling of his aging face. I could see him making eye contact with my attorney as if they already knew one another. The familiarity that flashed across their eyes was evident as they cracked upon their lips the slightest of smirks. It could have been a smile or a warning. Although neither was apparent. Looking beyond the man with the briefcase was a tall man in a black suit with a blue and gray tie. His wavy blonde hair fell down around his dazzling green eyes. When his eyes met mine, many things went through my mind and its difficult to sum them all up in words because they wouldn't do the feeling any justice. The tightening in my neck intensified as if an invisible boa constrictor were squeezing the life out of me. The familiarity that shone our eyes was different than that of the attorneys. Perhaps we had battled before, but we had conquered together and that was bond of its own uniqueness. My eyes widened at the sight of him, unable to laugh nor cry. My heart pounded in my chest, rattling me beyond comprehension. His eyes widened at me as if the feelings were mutual. As they made their way over the plaintiff side of the courtroom and seated themselves, our eyes never left one another. My breath quickened into hyperventilation as my attorney made every attempt to calm me down.

"Liza what's the matter?" he whispered to me as I extended my arms, placing my head down and looking at the floor.

"It's, It's him," I said in a panic.

"Who? Who is it Liza? What do you mean?" he whispered.

"All rise for the honorable Judge Stephenson," I heard a voice say.

My attorney pulled me by the arm, grabbing me up out of my seat. I kept my head down with a heavy breath as the roar of chatter grew silent.

"Mr. Andrews," I heard an old mans voice say. "Is your client alright? I don't have time for this today. Either get her under control or I am going to recess for the day. Do you understand me?"

"Yes sir," he replied, rubbing my back and urging me to collect my emotions.

I arose to the judge as my head perked up again. Then, moving my eyes across the room, over at Mr. Finkleman, I raised my hand to point at him.

"It's him!" I shouted. "It's him!"

"That's enough now Ms. Ward. If you continue with your outburst, I will hold you in contempt of court," the Judge warned.

Mr. Finkleman's eyes were frightened like a deer in in the headlights, paralyzed by the experience. As I lunged forward toward my dearest friend, an arm caught me in the crossfire, holding me back as I cried out for him.

"Stark!" I exclaimed. "Stark it's me. It's me, Liza!"

Tears rushed down my face as he looked upon me, but didn't react or make any kind of move. My heart was crushed by this rejection. What if he had no idea who I was?

"Stark please!" I yelled, trying to fight off the strong grips of hands that were holding me back.

He only sat there, looking up at me in disbelief. They must have thought I was crazy and was doing nothing to refute it. I could feel the chill of cold handcuffs clasping around my wrists as I was being yanked by my arms from behind. As I was being pulled further from his line of sight, I persisted in pleas for him to remember me. My character was being made into mockery. I felt he had abandoned me to experience the dark memories alone even though he so obviously remembered. Where was the Stark who fought to the death for me? As I screamed his name one last time, the officer drug me out of the courtroom and into his squad car. I could see Stark standing outside still looking down at me from the cement stairs in front of the courtroom. His eyes shone with slight concern, but more troubling was the way he so obviously recognized me.

"Stark!" I yelled as tears rushed down my face.

"Hey, pipe down back there!" the officer said pounding on the divider window.

I finally stopped screaming for him as I could see it was nothing but counterproductive. With the officer slamming his fist against the window and Stark staring at me like an idiot, I quieted my lips. Putting my head down to look at my lap, I realized this was a fight I just couldn't win. Nobody was going to believe the hair-brained mixture of stories I had collected in my memory. He was alive and well, looking back at me with his human eyes. His very energy permeated into the the space between us reminding me that I was there. I had been a part of something very rare and special; a portal into an alternate universe. This is where Stark and I had met and found one another, overcoming all obstacles to make it to the other side. Issiryth's curse was supposed to be impossible; however, we had both found the means to defeat it. I may have been going to jail that day, but I knew beyond a shadow of a doubt that I hadn't imagined any of it. Stark was real in all senses of the word. He was real in my mind and real in our physical plane.

The victory of this realization alone helped me along in the booking process as they mashed my fingers on the ink, rolling them carefully along small strips of paper. They snapped my picture, capturing may face from two angles. I got through the process the best I knew how; with few words and a quiet surrender. As I bent down in front of the female officer, fully exposed in my nakedness, I should have felt humiliated. Instead, I felt a sense of accomplishment. The confirmation I had desired presented itself to me and I couldn't ignore this special gift. My lips managed to curl up on my face when the light bulb illuminated in my head. Standing up to look back at the officer who had quite obviously found nothing in her strip search.

"That will do, Ward," she said with a blank expression. "Put your clothes back on."

"Don't I have jail clothes or something?" I asked.

"Not now. You're going to the holding tank," she said handing me my clothes back.

I was then escorted to a cement holding cell surrounded by bars. There were about five other women of all shapes and sizes looking up at me as if they all had the shittiest of days themselves. I tried not to make eye contact with any of them, out of fear that they may find cause to pummel me. There was a large cement bench lining the wall and a toilet in the corner. How much lower could I be? I was trapped in this jail, away from my children and dying mother. The whole purpose of my court appearance was to save her and I had fucked it up. I slumped down on the bench next to a middle aged woman with greasy black and white hair. She was chewing on her thumb as if she were trying to pry the nail away from the skin. She then turned to look at me as if I were a ghost, gasping and pointing.

"You killed him didn't you!?" she exclaimed.

The other women in the cell stared at me, just awaiting my rebuttal to her accusation. I looked back at her with a puzzling despair, she pointed her finger in my face.

"You killed him you little bitch. You let him die," she said.

"N, No. I didn't. I would never do that," I said.

"Liar!" she yelled, slamming her hand down on the concrete.

The others surrounded me with stares of oppression.

"You're a fucking liar! Liar Liza!" she exclaimed raising her hands up to engage the others. Soon they were all joining in.

"Liar Liza!" they said in unison. "You liar Liza. You killed him!"

"No!" I exclaimed. "I didn't!"

I buried my head down in the concrete, placing my hands up over me, trying to cancel out the noise. Soon enough, their voices faded away into the distance where all I could make out was a small semblance of a murmur. The sounds of their voices quieted in my head as I drifted away into what must have been sleep. It didn't feel like sleep however. It was as if I had slipped in between death and life again, simply floating somewhere in limbo. I was just grateful to have escaped the chaos.

"Liza Ward," I heard a stern voice say.

In the darkness, behind my eyes, I could feel myself resting my head on someone's lap. My eyes were blurry as I strained to open them up. The fluorescent lights overhead were bright and blaring down at me. I struggled to open my eyes. I jolted up looking down over my shoulder to see the lady with the greasy hair staring back at me with a jack-o'-lantern smile. I pushed myself up off the cement bench. There was an officer standing at the door.

"Are you Liza?" he asked looking at me.

"Yes," I said pointing at myself.

"Congrats you made bail," he said unlocking the door.

"Who? Who was it that bailed me out?" I asked

"The gentleman wanted to remain anonymous. He said that you're an old friend of his," he replied.

"Was he bald?" I asked.

"No, but he did say he owed one you for saving him," he said.

"Stark!" I exclaimed.

The officer was silent as I was given my things back. I called Syble on my cell phone to come pick me up and she was happy to oblige, as usual. Thoughts of Stark raced through my head as I awaited her arrival. I wondered what his life was like here on earth. It was ironic that he had been so close by me the entire time. Although a relief to see him alive and well, I wondered why he didn't stick around to talk to me. We had so much to talk about, after all. Syble pulled up in front of me, looking over her sunglasses.

"What am I going to do with you?" she said shaking her head.

I lowered myself into her car as I hung my head.

"I'm sorry about all this," I whispered.

"It's okay doll," she said putting her hand on my knee. "What happened?"

"I had an outburst in the courtroom," I said as I shifted in my seat.

"Oh Liza, no, please no," she said shaking her head. "Why?"

"I, I saw him. It was him," I said. She grabbed my chin, forcing me to look up at her.

"Who Liza? Is this another fantasy story? You allowed your fantasy story to land in you jail?" she asked.

"I saw him with my own eyes!" I exclaimed. "It's him! He's alive!"

She let out a deep sigh.

"Okay fine Liza. I give up. Who?" she asked throwing her hands in the air.

"Stark. He's the one who helped me turn into the mermaid so that I could get to Issiryth's island," I said.

"Isn't he the one that took you over there in the first place?" she asked.

"No, that was Blane," I responded.

"You had two love interests in your coma? That's so right out of the movies and into your head Liza. Are you being serious right now? I can't believe you made a fool of yourself," she said.

"I saw him though Syble. It's him. It's Stark. He's Virgil Finkleman!" I said.

"What? Virgil Finklemen?" she asked

"Yes, the guy who took mom to court. It was the same guy. Except in Sedania he was Stark," I said.

"Wait a second? You mean to tell me the guy in the green truck was Stark and you went to the alternate universe together?" she asked.

"Yes, that's exactly what I'm saying," I responded. She shook her head.

"Alright. That's it! You can't talk the rest of the way home. I'm done with this shit," she said.

"But...." I started

"Shhh," she responded quieting my lips with her finger.

We said nothing the entire ride home, but it was just as well.

I had enough to worry and think over anyhow. Her silence in the car reiterated her disgust toward my ramblings. I had to accept that this was something I would have to keep to myself. Surely when I found Stark again he would understand and give me his valuable insight. It was the only hope I had. The car came to a screeching halt in front of my apartment. Syble motioned for me to get out of the car. I dared not speak another word to her. So I simply tipped my head down in an attempt to show her gratitude for the ride home. I hung my head in shame as I walked up the steps and entered my apartment as she sped away.

"Virgil Finkleman," I whispered to myself trying to think of a way to contact him.

As I rose up the to the top of the steps, turning the shiny doorknob, it hit me. He hadn't spoken up for me because he wanted me to look crazy. *He wanted me to lose. Didn't he?* I thought. I reached down in my purse, fishing out my cell phone. It was 3 o'clock and soon my kids would be home on the school bus. I was relieved my time in jail was short lived enough to have avoided another setback with my children, but I feared my troubles were just beginning. As I looked at the smooth glass face of my phone, it illuminated with the name of my attorney as it sang a song of expectation.

"Answer me," it said. "Answer me or you'll regret it."

"Hello," I said.

"Liza, what was that all about? I heard you got out of jail. Are you alright?" my attorney asked.

"Yes, I'm alright. Will we be able to get a new court date?" I asked.

"Well, I talked to Mr. Finkleman's attorney and he said that he wants to drop the whole thing. He's taking most of the fault in the accident," he said.

"What?" my heart fluttered with excitement. "He does?"

"Yes, Liza. I know you're an attractive woman, but your sexual power even surprises me at times," he said.

"What's that supposed to mean? I didn't have sex with him!" I snapped back.

"I'm not saying you did, but it seems like the two of you recognized each other and he's suddenly ready to drop it all. I'm just wondering how you did it and that's the only conclusion I can draw," he said.

"No, I don't know him. At least I don't I think I do," I said.

"Well, never mind what I said. Your mom was in a for a hell of a lawsuit if he had followed through with it. So, we got what we wanted either way. Can you be at my office in the morning? He and his lawyer have agreed to meet with us to iron things out. There's an insurance claim too of course, but we've agreed that neither one of you will do statements with them until we've all sat down together," he said.

"Okay, yes, I suppose that's fine. Will I be able to talk to Virgil?" I asked hoping he would say yes. I had to speak to Stark again no matter what.

"Well, no Liza. Not really. I mean, I suppose if you meet in the hallway you can say hello, but it's important that you allow the counselors to handle this. You don't want him to change his mind," he advised.

"Okay, I guess you're right. Thanks for your help. I'll see you tomorrow," I replied.

"Okay kiddo. Take care," he said.

Click. The phone disconnected with so many rushing thoughts flowing through me like a river. This was my opportunity to talk to Stark, but under the circumstances, I wasn't quite sure how that would work out. I couldn't torment over that just now, but rather be still in the moment. I was thankful for another day with my boys. It was another day to be alive and aware on this earth to project and express myself in all my positive qualities. I was Liza Ward; a mom, worker, friend, and daughter. I reminded myself daily that I was who I was and I would again wake up every time I laid my head on the pillow to the night's slumber. It was a blessing I would never again take for granted.

CHAPTER 6
UNTO HIS ARMS I SHALL RETURN

Years ago, when I sat at my father's side, holding his hand as he lie dying his hospital bed, he looked up at me with warm eyes. They say our eyes are the window to our soul and I can attest that this is truth. While his body withered away into death's arms, there was no hurt, judgment , or revenge. All of those human emotions that consume us in our lives, whittled down into acceptance. In that moment when you know that life has passed you by, all that remains are the memories. Memories can either haunt or bless you, depending on how you've lived your life. I couldn't cry in that moment when my father took his last breath because I didn't want these precious moments to be experienced in grief. My mom always said I had the uncanny ability to smile and tap dance when chaos was rearing its ugly head at me. Perhaps at times she viewed this as a negative, but it was how I had learned to cope with life. In tears, I was admitting defeat and I didn't want the display of them to upset the others around me. I didn't think that allowing life to get the better of me was a viable option.

"I love you Liza. Life will bring you great things," he said.

At the time, my belly was giant and protruding out with pregnancy. He never did get to meet Jameson, but he knew that I would be a good mother. He believed in me at least. I felt he may have been disappointed with the way I gave my heart away, hoping that Jace would be there to pick up the pieces. My father had left me, after all. Perhaps it was not of his own will, but I still felt the painful tinge of abandonment anyhow. It's a bit embarrassing to admit, but even the smallest touch of the arm or gaze from Jace made the pang of my father's absence a little more bearable. I resented my dad for dying even though it wasn't his fault. It wasn't fair, but it was how I felt. When his hand grew limp and the life left his body, it was then that I allowed my tears to come out, but only for a small moment. My mother couldn't be troubled with my grief either. She had enough of her own to deal with. I suppose it was my father's death that caused me to question to my own validity. I was always trying to fill a hole that could never be filled.

With the memory of my father weighing heavily on my heart that day, I pulled up to the tall off white building where my attorney housed his office. Driving into the dark parking garage, I took several deep breaths in anticipation for my confrontation with Stark. *What would I do? What would I say?* Surely he knew me as I had seen the expression of familiarity in his eyes when I saw him. Even though I had been advised not to speak with him, how could I hold back? He had been such an intricate part of my life, or so I thought he had been. The realness of my world was indeed questionable, but I couldn't allow that to stop me in my quest for answers.

I grasped my purse by the straps, with the tight grasp of fists clenched around it. I picked up my cell phone a few times, but kept placing it back down again. I was thirty minutes early and this time to spare proved to be a breeding ground for anxiety. I didn't want to feel rejected by Stark again. He could easily dismiss me if he wanted to because he didn't owe me anything at all. My mind recoiled over the time when I watched him die on the beach. Just like my father, he had warm eyes free from any vengeance. He only had acceptance for his inevitable fate. That "I love you" that managed to escape his lips must have been love in it's purest form. He had nothing to gain in saying it because he knew he was going to die. There was no reward or prize at the end. It was said only for me and my benefit, as his gap of time between life and death grew smaller until it was closed. I knew his sentiment must have been genuine and I wondered if he had heard mine before he drifted away. This alone reconciled within my heart that Stark must have truly loved me.

I opened my car door, slinging my purse up over my shoulder. I held my head high and forced a smile. It was time for me to tap dance now. I would go into this pretending that his reaction didn't matter to me. I made my way down out of the parking garage and into the lobby of the building. In front of me, I could see tall man in a suit with short blonde hair. His back was turned to me, but his figure was bold and statuesque. He pressed the up button on the elevator as I stood behind him unseen awaiting the the bulb on the elevator to light up so that we could step on. His foot tapped against the the ceramic tile flooring. I had the urge to tap him on the shoulder and turn him around to see who I was looking at, but my nerve didn't allow it. I knew this must have been Stark with a new business-like haircut, but I couldn't take my chances on looking like an idiot.

The elevator managed to light up and open its doors so that we could make our voyage to the sixth floor. He stepped on with a cell phone lifted to his ear as if he were calling someone, not really paying attention to me following behind him. He kept his head turned away from me. Perhaps he had been on some kind of important phone call. As he turned to the side, I immediately recognized that my assertion was true. I pushed the button as the elevator doors closed. I took a deep breath in and out, just trying to maintain composure. He turned to face me His shimmering green eyes met mine as his hand grew weak and limp, dropping the cell phone to the floor. His jaw dropped down as his eyes widened in surprise.

"Oh my God! Stay away from me!" he said.

"Stay away from you? Don't you know who I am?" I asked. My heart was racing.

"I don't know what's going on here, but I'm not playing games with you," he said backing into the corner of the elevator.

In a moment of impulsivity, I reached over to the emergency button pressing the large red circle in order to stop it. Alarms bells began sounding off in the small box as he placed his hands out in front of himself to stop me from approaching.

"I'm not playing games with you Stark. How can you act like this after all we've been through together?" I asked approaching him, yet keeping my distance.

"This is just fucked up. It's all fucked up. It was just a dream. It's not real," he said.

"I know. I keep trying to convince myself of the same thing, but here we are," I said giving him a deep stare. My brown eyes widened at him.

Each of us had a heavy rhythmic breath as we stared into one another with the flush of intensity and heat. I reached up and touched his hands, wrapping my fingers around them as I gently pulled down. I squeezed each of his hands in mine, pulling his body closer. He was silent for a moment as he put his hand to my face, pulling the hair back out of my eyes and tucking it behind my ear.

"It's not like I have a thing for you. You know?" he said with a grin. "But I am glad to see you Liza. I don't know what all of this means. I'm a very logical person."

"I don't know what it means either, but there's something going on. I have nobody to talk to who would understand. He's real Stark. He showed me the portal again," I said.

"You're bullshitting right?" he responded.

"No, I'm not bullshitting you. Every time I say his name, the ground shakes. My kids have been talking about a woman they call Izzy who visits them in their sleep," I began to ramble. "You're the only one who would believe me."

"How's your mother?" he asked changing the subject and staring off at the wall.

"She's still in a coma. They want me to pull the plug on her," I said with a gulp in my chest.

"He has her," he said looking back down at me. "He has her and he wont give her back until he has you."

"So, she'll wake up. She'll wake up just like you and I did," I responded.

"We only woke up because we betrayed him and went to the forbidden island. There's no way he's ever letting anyone cross ever again. Your mom is his prisoner now. He wont give her back unless you sacrifice yourself," he said.

"But I can't do that. I have to be here for my boys," I said.

"Then I suggest you pull the plug. Don't let him defeat you Liza. You're stronger than him," he said.

"If I'm stronger than he is, then I can get her back. How do you know I don't want to be with him? I loved him and he loved me," I said.

"Don't be a fool Liza. He used you just like he uses everyone. I swear if I ever go into a coma again, I'd rather meet the devil himself," he said.

"Don't say that. You can help me just as you did before. I know how to make the portal appear. I have to save Mom. She has to wake up again. If I crossed the boundary once, I can do it again," I said.

"There is no way you're getting me to go into that damn thing again," he said.

"But we have to," I said furrowing my brow. "I can't pull the plug on my mom's life. I watched my father die and I watched you die. I can't watch her die. You don't understand. Please help me," I begged. His eyes grew soft and gentle.

"You know I'd do anything for you kiddo, but I can't deal with that son of a bitch again. He'd kill me as soon as he saw me with you anyway. He feels threatened by me, as if I will take you away from him," he said.

"I know, but we're just friends right? We can explain that to him. He loves me. He wont hurt you if he knows you're a friend that I care about," I said.

"Do you hear yourself? This isn't just a guy you've dated! He's some sort of alien! He abides by a different set of rules! He's more foreign than you can pretend to understand," he yelled. His arms clasped around my shoulders as he drew close to me.

I stood there still facing him so closely that our noses barely touched. I could feel his body pressing against mine as his breath grazed across my skin like a warm summer breeze. The strength of his grasp got me wet inside my panties and his eyes had me lost in a realm of temptation. My heart pounded in my chest like bulldozer. I could feel my palms growing clammy from the intensity. I closed my eyes awaiting the greeting of warm soft lips enveloping mine with his lust. The sexual tension was mounting as I could feel his heart beating through his chest with an equal ferocity to mine.

"We're just friends," he said resting his forehead on mine and extending his arms outward to place me away from him. "I'm sorry I got out of control just now."

"It's okay," I said. "I can't do this without you. You're the only one who understands."

"Let me think about it okay? I have to think about all of this," he said in a low whisper.

"Okay," I nodded. "I suppose that's fair. I'm glad you're okay."

I squeezed his hand.

"Me too Liza. I'm happy to be alive and well. Trust me," he responded.

"How's your family? Are they happy you're back?" I asked.

"Yes, of course," he said trying to cut the conversation short, but I continued to prod him.

"I thought your name was Stark. What is this Virgil Finklemen business? It sounds like something out of a movie depicting a nerd-boy," I teased.

"Virgil, was my grandfather's name," he responded, not amused. "Stark is my middle name. Nobody dared call me Virgil Finkleman growing him, but it is my legal name."

"Oh, I'm sorry," I giggled.

"Yeah, I know. Get a good laugh. You're lucky you're a girl," he snapped.

"I'm sorry Stark. Okay? I'll stop," I said. He rolled his eyes.

"You know with my family being so far away all of this has been really hard to deal with," he said. My cheeks blushed with color.

"What about your girlfriend?" I fished.

"I don't have a girlfriend. I was pretty clear with you that I don't do that sort of thing," he responded.

"Well, I guess I just assumed you had one here. That's all," I said.

"Well you know what happens when you assume," he said tilting his head at me.

He pulled the fire alarm out, stopping the obnoxious ringing and bringing the elevator back into motion. We could see the lights moving as we reached the sixth floor. I moved my hand into his, squeezing it as if to say I never wanted to let him go. He looked over at me, then down at our connected hands, letting a small smile pass his lips. Again facing forward, he didn't ward off my affection. The elevator dinged as the doors opened up to our attorneys standing side-by-side. Their puzzled eyes looked at us in amazement as they looked down to see the two of us holding hands as we stepped off. In the realization that the two of us had come to this place together to combat one another, we released our grip. Each going our separate directions, my attorney swooped me off by the small of my back.

"Could you excuse us for a moment?" he said addressing the gentlemen.

"Of course," his attorney responded, then whispered something to Stark in his ear.

Alone in the office now with my attorney, he looked my body up and down like a dirty old man ogling over a busty school girl. The way he undressed me with his eyes was more obvious than python in a bucket of worms, but I would pretend not to notice.

"You look great Liza. You really do," he said licking his lips.

"Thank you," I responded sitting down.

"You're hot, but I seriously wonder where your head is," he

began to reprimand. "I told you that you could say hello, not hold him captive in the elevator and try to make him your boyfriend."

"He's not my boyfriend. It's just that we know each other," I said.

"You know each other? You told me you didn't know him," he questioned.

"I don't know him, know him. I just thought I knew him, but I guess he was more of just someone who I've passed by before you know?" I said, talking in circles. He looked at me sideways.

"Okay, it's going to take a miracle for this guy not to mutilate you legally speaking at this point. You've made a fool of yourself," he said.

"I know that. Just do what you can okay? My mother can't have a lawsuit as soon as she wakes up," I said.

"Okay Liza," he said, rising up out of his seat. "You stay here. I'm going to go talk to Mr. Finkleman's attorney for a moment. I'll be back okay?"

"Okay," I nodded, getting out my phone and beginning to click the apps.

I sat in his office for what felt like an eternity, but the clock was telling me a different story. It had only been about five minutes before he appeared again to tell me the news.

"He wants to drop everything Liza," he said.

The relief set in knowing that this would soon be behind me. I could feel my tense muscles relieving back into ease. Seeing Stark confirmed a new set problems though. Sedania was a real place and my mother may be trapped there. I knew I had quite a journey in my future.

"Okay, that's great," I said as I put my phone on the table.

"Can I talk to him now?"

"If you want to, but I think he got a work call. He's already left," he said.

"Oh no! Are you sure?"

"Yeah.. I'm pretty sure," he said.

"I have to talk to him. It's important! I have to go!" I yelled.

"I just need you to stay for a bit so we can go over the paperwork," he responded.

"Okay, okay," I said snatching the pen from his fingers and scratching my signature on each sheet of paper.

Without another word, I made a b-line for the elevators seeing a sign on the door for the stairwell. I couldn't afford to wait for the elevator to rise up to the appropriate floor as every minute was precious. I flung the door open and sprinted down the staircase as quickly as my legs could carry me. With each flight of stairs, my legs pumped beneath me, propelling me forward with each step. My breath grew strong and heavy as the exertion gave my body a run for it's money. My throbbing legs pressed on, carrying me down each flight of stairs. I rounded the corner of the bottom step of the lowest level, tearing open the door to the lobby. I could see his blonde head turned away from me with his cell phone pressed to his ear.

"Stark!" I huffed, collapsing my torso down to rest my hands on my knees as I caught my breath. "Please wait!"

He turned around to look at me. He dropped his cell phone from his ear as he ended the call.

"I was going to come back and give you my phone number," he said laughing. "You're kind of cute all out of breath like that."

I rolled my eyes, still doubled over in hyperventilation.

"Okay, just give me your number," I huffed, holding my cell phone out to him.

He grabbed it out of my hands and began typing away. I could see his eyes were in contemplative thought. He wrinkled his eyebrows.

"Who's Gary?" he asked holding it up in front of my face.

"Give me that," I said grabbing it out of his hands.

"Is that your boyfriend? Your earth boyfriend?"

"No... well, sort of, but I dumped him."

"You dumped him?" he asked. He rubbed the bottom of his chin. "Interesting."

"Why is that interesting?" I responded.

"Because nobody breaks up with their boyfriend unless they have someone else," he said.

"I beg your pardon?" I said raising my eyebrows at him.

"You heard me. You have what's his name now. You don't want your boyfriend anymore. It's so obvious to me. You're so that type," he said.

"You have no idea what type I am Virgil!" I rebutted. I could see his eyes turning red. He balled up his fists and barred his teeth. Every muscle in his body tensed.

"Yes, I do. I know exactly what type you are and I could have you if I wanted," he reminded me.

"You wish," I said. His green eyes peered back at me. I could see I had struck a nerve. *Perhaps I shouldn't have used his real name.* I thought.

"Thank you for bailing me out."

His eyes narrowed as he released his fists. His posture began to relax again. He shifted back and forth on his feet.

"I'll see you later Liza. Call me tomorrow," he said. His heels clicked against the concrete of the parking lot as he pressed the phone back up to his ear and walked away.

Perhaps I should have been bothered by his cold departure, but I wasn't. I was ecstatic to have someone in my corner who understood. The love I had for him was confusing. On one hand he was a great friend. On the other, I had feelings for Blane that I could not reconcile in my heart. Stark had made it pretty clear that he doesn't do the whole boyfriend and girlfriend thing. Blane had made it pretty clear that he was controlling. I was always searching for something inside of me. There was always a longing. There was a space that could only be filled with the love of a man. Why was I this way? It seemed as if they both used it against me. Who was the man who could fill the void? Was it Stark or Blane?

CHAPTER 7

LET'S GO

The cold water surrounded my feet with relief as I soaked them in the pool on that hot Texas day. The boys splashed about in the water, only coming out to get a drink or declare a noodle war. Any way they could get a slap in, whether fair or unfair, they would. They were still as loud and rambunctious as before making me think this new normal was not quite as hard on them as I might have believed. The slap of the the foam on my son's bare skin resounded in the air with an echo The piercing, shrill scream, penetrated my head as if a needle were being shoved right through my skull.

"Guys, stop it," I said. "I'm going to take those things away from you if you don't."

"No!!" they whined in unison returning to their water games.

"Here you go," Syble said, handing me an ice-cold glass of lemonade.

"Thanks," I said, sipping the contents of the glass. Syble sat next to me, placing her feet in the water . Her perky breasts sat in the top of her bathing suit, reminding me of the havoc motherhood had taken on my body. Her perfect abs shimmered in the summer sun. Her stomach didn't roll when she sat, but rather it all displaced perfectly. It made her look like a Goddess.

"Yikes, that's cold. I don't understand how the kids don't feel it," she said. Her feet retracted backward.

"I know, but they don't care if it's not even summer yet. They just want to swim. It's warm enough today I guess," I shrugged.

"You know, only you could look so good in a bikini after two kids and third on the way," she said looking at me. I could feel the small twinge of jealousy welling up inside. How could she even think that? She looked perfect. I was already starting to look bloated.

"Well, I just found out," I laughed. "The baby is like the size of a marble or something."

"God, I hope I look as good as you when I have kids," she said. I cracked a smile.

"You know, you did things the right way not getting married. Look at you. You have this awesome house with a pool and nobody to worry about, but your little dogs... and look at you. Your body is perfection" I responded.

"Oh please... and in all fairness, I inherited a lot of money from my grandmother," she said.

"Okay, I guess you're right, but still. Love sucks. I wish I could be strong like you," I said. I squinted my eyes as the sun caught them. I placed my hand over my forehead, casting a shadow over my eyes.

"There's no right or wrong way to do things Liza. We're all on a different journey. You know? By the way, how did things go with your lawyer and the Finkleman guy?" she asked. I knew Syble had kind intentions, but if she was going to dismiss the things I said, why was she prompting me in the first place? I knew she didn't want to hear that Stark acknowledged me and the islands. So, I choose my words carefully.

"He's dropping everything. He's going to leave mom and her assets alone," I responded. Her face lit up at the news.

"That's great! I can't believe you got him to drop everything! How did you do it? Did you seduce him or something?" she asked. I swallowed, knowing again that I would have to choose my words carefully.

"Don't be silly," I said rolling my eyes. "I suppose Mr. Finkleman is just a reasonable man after all."

"Well, I'm glad all that's behind you. Now, you just need to focus on getting your mom better," she said. *I am.* I thought to myself. *I'm going to do everything within my power to get my mom better and that would involve going back to face Blane again.* Although I so deeply wanted to see him, I knew that doing so could have some unforeseen consequences. My phone rang on the table and illuminated with Stark's name. My belly fluttered with a rush of excitement. As I sprang from my place by the pool to answer it, the eye of suspicion was upon me. Syble pursed her lips with a questioning expression.

"I have to take this," I said picking up the phone. I closed the sliding glass door behind me as I shuffled into the house. The cool, air conditioned air swept across my skin as I stepped out of the heat. I scurried down the long dark hallway to the bathroom, where I shut and locked the door behind me.

"Hello."

"Hey," Stark's voice said. "What are you doing?"

"The kids and I are at Syble's house swimming. Well, the kids are swimming. What are you doing?" I asked.

"I've just been thinking about everything. Can I see you today?" he asked.

"Um, I don't know yet. Only if Syble agrees to watch the kids I guess," I responded.

"Okay. I'll come pick you up. Where are you?" he said.

"You want the address? You're coming to pick me up now?" I asked.

"Yea, I'm coming to get you now. Tell your friend you're going to leave town for a few days."

"What? Stark, I can't do that. Is she supposed to just take that as okay when I have to handle mom being in the hospital and all that?" I asked.

"You have to Liza. How else are we going to get your mother back?" he asked.

"You mean you're going to help me? You're going to go with me?"

"Well, the idea of dying a painful death again isn't all that appealing, but I thought about it and we're in this thing together. "

"What am I supposed to tell Syble? She just had the kids while I was in a coma. I can't just tell her I'm going on vacation. That would be highly inappropriate under the circumstances."

"Why don't you just tell me where you are? I can handle this," he said.

"Well, okay, but I don't think she's going to go for it. I'm on 4235 Burch Street," I said.

"Okay, be there in about 10 minutes," he said before disconnecting the call. I put my phone down on the counter top. My insides were churning. I wrapped my arms around my belly and sat down on the toilet lid. My eyes peered up at the ceiling. *What am I doing?* I thought to myself. *Maybe I should just pull the plug. Mom wouldn't want to live like this. Blane wasn't real. Was he?*

Bang, bang, bang.... I could hear Syble's fist smashing against the bathroom door.

"Liza, are you alright? Who was that who called you?" she asked. I opened the bathroom door to have a look at her, conflicted about the answer I would give. I could feel tears forming in my red eyes, but I labored to hold them back.

"It was nobody," I said, looking away.

"I can always tell when you're lying. Your eyes are so big and expressive, you always give yourself away. You can't bullshit a bullshitter my love," she said.

"If I were to tell you, you wouldn't believe me," I said.

"Oh, let me guess. It was Blane right? Blane called to say he wants you to come back to never-land right?" she teased.

"No, it wasn't Blane," I shook my head defensively.

"Oh, it must have the been the other one then right? Virgil?" she asked.

"Yes," I whispered quietly still looking away from her.

"You're kidding right? Liza, am I going to have to have you committed?" she asked.

"See, I knew I shouldn't have said anything. He's on his way over here. You can meet him yourself," I responded.

"What? Why is he coming over here?" she asked.

"To pick me up," I responded.

"To pick you up? Where are you guys going? What about the kids?" she asked. I blinked, again giving her a wide-eyed expression. She shook her head.

"You know I love the boys, but its polite to ask someone if they can watch them not just assume."

"Listen Syble, this is important. I wouldn't ask you if it weren't important. He'll be here soon and he'll tell you himself," I said. She nodded placing her hand around my shoulder and leading me down the hallway. A rush of warm air hit us as she slid open the sliding glass door to the backyard. She had the boys all set up with popsicles, sitting on the patio furniture. The red dye had colored their lips and teeth as they devoured them.

"Mom, where did you go? Will you swim with us?" asked Noah.

"Not now honey, mom has a friend stopping by for a minute," I responded. He frowned.

"Is it a man?" he asked.

"Yes," I replied. "Just a friend of mine."

"Oh," he said, turning to grab his brother by the arm. The noodle wars resumed as they splashed in the water. I hated to disappoint my children especially after everything I had gone through to get back to them. It wasn't fair that a man was again preoccupying my time and taking me away. All the boys knew was that mom woke up from a coma. They had no understanding of the toll it had actually taken on me. They expected me to be back to normal, but I never would be again. Ding, went my phone.

"He's here," I said with a flirtatious smirk.

"Well, you better go let him in," she rolled her eyes.

The rush of cold air tickled my skin as I went back through the house. The excitement reached up inside of me. I knew he was standing there on the other side of the door. I began to adjust my hair as I peered into a nearby hanging mirror. I saw how the sun had started to flush my cheeks with a rosy coloration. I wondered if he would still find my look appealing. I opened the front door. He was standing there wearing blue jeans with flip-flops with a plaid button up shirt. His sleeves were rolled to his elbows. I could see the freckles on his arms, which were accented by bulging veins. His muscles stood out from beneath his shirt. He put his sunglasses on top of his head as he looked down at me with his beautiful eyes. In that moment I forgot that that I was dressed in my bathing suit. I could see his green eyes scanning my body. The black bikini I was wearing had barely covered the unmentionables. He was noticeably salivating as the sight of me. He put his hand to the back of his head and raised his eyebrows. I flung my arms around his neck.

"I'm so glad you're here," I whispered in his ear.

"Me too," he said, placing his hands around my tiny waste to pull me in closer to him. His breath warmed my neck and shoulders. In his tight grip, I could feel the strength and safety of his arms. I pulled away, peering into his green eyes.

"Wanna meet Syble?" I asked.

"Sure."

I tugged his hand, pulling him through the house. I slid open the back door. Syble was sitting at the side of the pool with her feet in the water. She was watching the boys as they raced one another across the pool. Each of them was demonstrating their best backstroke.

"Syble this is Stark," I said. She jumped as she looked up at him. Her eyes widened at him. He extended out his hand to as she rose up to shake it.

"It's nice to meet you Stark," she said.

"Likewise," he said walking over to the side of the pool. He knelt down next to Noah and Jameson. "And who might you fellows be?"

"I'm Noah, this is my brother Jameson!" Noah responded. I could see Syble mouthing the words 'he's hot' from behind him. I nodded in agreement.

"It's nice to meet you guys. How old are y'all?" he asked.

"I'm 8 said Jameson. I'm the oldest," Jameson said proudly.

"I'm almost 7. My birthday is in two months," said Noah.

"I see. Well what are y'all doing out here? Noodle wars?" he asked.

"Yea, do you want to play?" Noah asked.

"Maybe next time. Y'all have fun okay?" he said

"Okay!" they said in unison. The pleasant exchange between Stark and the boys was a bit unexpected. He didn't seem like he even liked children, but there he was interacting with mine like a champ. Syble and I had situated ourselves on the patio furniture. He turned to us.

"Can I get you a drink?" she asked.

"No thanks," he said waving his hands in front of him. "I've come to take Liza away for a few days. Do you think you can manage with the boys?" he asked.

"Stark!" I exclaimed.

"It's okay Liza," she said putting her hand on my arm. "Where are you taking her?"

"To the islands of Sedania to get her mother back from Blane," he said. The utter look of shock shown across her face. Her eyes widened at him. She stood up and tensed her muscles.

"Don't tell me you buy this shit too. Liza's mother is in a coma," she said.

"Liza and I were there whether you believe us or not. That's how we met each other. Her mother is still in his world. This is important. Do you understand?" his voice was sharp and commanding.

"So, I mean....What are you guys going to do? Slip back into a coma by your own will?" she asked.

"Liza knows how to get to the portal. I assume we'll appear to be asleep here in this world," he said.

"I wasn't going to tell her about that," I said looking at him.

"You know how to make the portal appear?" she asked. She rolled her eyes.

"Yes, I think so," I said. "I haven't perfected it or anything."

"So, I'm just supposed to take the boys for a couple of days while the two of you slip into a deep sleep to rescue your mother from a crazy man in an alternate universe?" she asked tilting her head to the side.

"Yes," we said in unison nodding at her. She tilted her head to the other side as she pressed her finger to her temple.

"Well, okay. You two kids have fun," she said. She winked at me before grabbing her glass of lemonade from the table. She lifted the bottom of the glass to the sky as she swallowed every last drop of it. I was bit surprised by her willingness.

"I'm tired of fighting you on this Liza. I think some time away would do you good."

"It's no vacation. Trust me," I responded.

"Okay well when are y'all planning to head out?" she asked.

"As soon as possible," Stark said.

"Okay then," she nodded.

"Okay then," I said getting up to approach the boys who

were still playing in the water.

"Boys get out. Mommy has to tell you something."

The boys swam to the side of the pool. The water splashed beneath their feet as they stepped out onto the hot concrete. They looked at me with the wide eyes of anticipation.

"Guys, I'm going away for a few days and you're going to stay here with your aunt Syble," I said.

"No mommy," Noah whined. "Why can't you stay here?"

"Because I have to save Grandma. That's why," I said.

"You're going to save Grandma?" Jameson asked.

"Yes, my friend Stark and I are going to save her and she's going to wake up again just like mommy did. Isn't that wonderful?" I asked.

"I guess so," Jameson said with a frown.

"Listen guys, I'm going to be back and everything is going to be fine okay? Pound on it?" I said extending my fist. The boys reluctantly gave me a fist bump.

I hugged them each planting warm kisses on their face. My heart sank. Leaving them was heart wrenching, but at the same time, I knew I had to save my mom. The state she was in was beyond the realm of medical intervention. I had to to penetrate Blane's world and coax her from the inside out.

"Are you ready to go?" Stark said looking at me. I nodded, slipping on my flip-flops and wrapping a towel around my waist. Outside, parked there in front of Syble's house, was a brand new silver Mercedes Benz. I gasped, but tried to conceal my surprise as he opened the door for me. When he put the key in the ignition, a screen popped up showing every angle of his blind spots. This car was certainly indicative of man who had experienced a great deal of success in his lifetime. As I buckled my seatbelt, I could feel a tear slipping out from beneath my eyelid.

"What's wrong?" Stark asked.

"I just didn't want to leave them ever again," I said in a low voice.

"You're not leaving them Liza. You're just going to get your mother," he comforted.

It didn't seem to help, however, as I knew that this discomfort would persist in my journey no matter how many times I told myself that I was well intended.

"Where are we going?" I asked.

"Somewhere where we can rest our heads," he responded.

"Well, I'm in a bathing suit. Do you mind if I go home and change?" I asked.

"Trying to get me back to your place already?" he teased. I popped his arm with my fist.

"You wish," I said.

"That's fine," he laughed. "If you're more comfortable there, that's probably where we should try to enter the portal anyway.

"Okay, well I'm down on Harwell Avenue. It's the old shoe store on the corner," I said motioning with my finger in the general direction of my home.

"You live in a shoe store?" he asked.

"I live in the apartment over the shoe store, yes," I said.

"Really? That's really cute Liza. You run a shoe store?" he asked.

"Cute is for puppies," I said rolling my eyes. "It was my dad's, I took it over when he died."

"I'm sorry you lost your dad. How did he die?" he asked.

"He had stomach cancer. He died a couple of months after we found out. It was already in stage four," I shrugged.

"I'm really sorry Liza. It must be hard for you trying to raise two boys without your dad around especially because you don't have a----," he stopped himself.

" A what? A husband?" I asked looking up at him with my big brown eyes. He looked back with a gentle sincerity.

"Yea I guess I was going to say husband, but you're a strong woman. I'm sure you're doing a great job without one. Your boys look like they're doing well," he responded.

"Yes, they are. Thank you. Mom and Syble help me a lot. It takes a village. You know?" I said.

"Yea, I get that. Have they ever met any of your boyfriends?" he asked.

"A few," I sighed. "But nobody has worked out so far. I think it's better if the three of us just try to go at it alone from now on. It's too much trouble."

"Don't say that Liza," he said squeezing my knee. The feel of his hand gave me a bit of a stir in the midst of our conversation. "You're a great catch. Any guy would be an idiot not to fall head over heels in love with you and your kids."

Looking at him with a soft expression, I placed my hand on top of his and pressed it down into my knee. His words sank in to me like an anchor in the ocean. He believed that I was lovable and that my children were too. How could he look at my situation and think it was desirable when so many others had passed me by because of it? He must have seen something in me that others didn't and his sentiment warmed my heart.

"Thanks," I said as we pulled into the parking spot behind my apartment. "Shall we go now?"

"Yes, of course. After you," he said motioning for me to get out of the car.

I pushed the door of the Mercedes open, careful not to compromise the luster of it. He got out and rushed to my side of the car to open the door for me.

"Thank you," I said with a look of suspicion. "You're awful gentleman-like."

"Of course," he said. "Let's go."

CHAPTER 8

HE DIDN'T SAY THREE

I carefully slipped the key into the keyhole of the door to my apartment. My back was turned to Stark, but I could feel the warmth of his body heat behind me. I still had my towel wrapped around my waist, but I could feel it slipping down. Soon my butt was the only thing holding it up. I rattled the door to try to get it ajar, but it stuck just a little. As I turned the door handle, I could feel the towel slipping down off of me. The bottoms of the bathing suit were sticking to the top of my bum, allowing my round cheeks to peak out the bottom at my spectator. The doorknob was turning, but the door wouldn't open for some reason. I pushed a bit more, but I was unsuccessful. I felt Stark's big hand stroke down my right arm as he placed his hand over mine. His left arm reached around my other side, pressing upon the door. His body surrounded me as he used his strength to force the door open. Once inside his body was still flush with mine as he swung the door shut with his foot.

We stood there, hushed by the intensity of our connection as his hands moved down around my waist. His nose smashed into my locks of chestnut brown hair as he inhaled, letting out a breath of desire. As his warm breath grazed my skin like a gentle breeze, he moved his hand down into the front of my bathing suit, hooking his finger into my clitoris. I became wet at his touch. Adrenaline was sweeping across my body like a wild fire. The hyper-beating of my heart caused my breath to quicken as his hand played my sex like a violin. Soon I could feel the wetness of his tongue on my neck as he kissed it. His other hand slid beneath my bathing suit top as he fondled my breast on their top. My nipples began to harden with his touch. I rolled my head to the side and began to moan, rocking my pelvis back and forth to the rhythm of fingers. He slid his finger deep into my vagina, pulling it out to take a taste, then shoving it back in again.

"Does that feel good Liza?" he asked.

"Yes," I moaned out loud.

"Do you want me stop? I'll stop if you want me to," he whispered.

"No, please don't stop," I begged.

He pushed me up against the back of couch, bending me over and taking the bottoms of my bathing suit down to my ankles. As he did so, he knelt down behind me, plunging his tongue into my pussy as his finger slid in and out of me. I could feel the pleasure sensations pulsating with a twinge that ran all the down my legs and into my toes. I moaned.

"Don't stop, please don't," I yelled out again.

He stood me up, placing his hands around my waist and turning my body around. He sat me up on the back of the couch. His fingers wrapped around the top of my thighs. He pried them open. He jammed his finger into me.

"God, your legs are so sexy," he said.

Our eyes met with a seductive gaze. He pulled his wet finger out and put it up to his nostril to inhale my scent. He placed it up against my plump lips.

"Taste yourself, Liza. You taste so good," he said.

I licked and sucked his salty finger as he fondled my breast with his other hand. Pulling my head in from behind, he kissed me. Our tongues danced a tango as I unbuttoned his shirt. Grabbing his collar with both hands, I pulled him over the back of the couch on top of me. I could feel his member bulging through his jeans, teasing me with its hardness. He began untying the top of my bathing suit and flinging off to the floor. His kisses made their way down my neck and on to my nipple, taking my whole breast in his hand as he bit it. The wetness between my thighs flowed like a river after a heavy rain as he continued to pleasure me with his finger. My fingers fumbles as I pulled open the buckle on his jeans.

"Take them off," I commanded.

"Yes 'mam," he said, revealing his big hard cock.

My hands grabbed each side of his hips, pulling his pro-truding member into my face. I grabbed hold of it, moving my tongue in circles around its head. I relaxed my throat, trying to take all of it in my mouth. *Ignore the gag reflex.* I told myself.

"Oh God, that feels so good!" he said gathering the hair out of my face and holding it in a bundle at the nape of my neck. I continued to move his cock in and out of my mouth as the saliva trickled down his shaft, creating lubrication for the other hand that was stroking it. When I could take it no more, I rose up to him, placing each hand on his pec muscles and pushing him down to a laying position on the couch. I straddled him, sliding my wet pussy down on his cock.

"Oh God," I yelled out grabbing each of my breasts in my own hands.

His penis fit like a puzzle inside of me as the walls of my vagina hugged him in a wet, slippery playground. Each breast bounced about as I slid up and down on him. He grabbed my ass in each hand, guiding my hips as we made love. I laid down on him. With my chest against his, we met with a passionate kiss. I felt him holding my body as he continued to pulse his dick in-side of me. I could feel myself close to orgasm; on the brink of explosion.

"I'm about to cum, make me cum Stark," I whispered in his ear.

"Yea baby, I'll make you cum," he said, pushing harder and faster inside of me.

"Oh God!" I exclaimed. "Oh God you're making me cum!"

His breath became hard and heavy as he finished inside of me. He slowed his rhythm to relieve himself. Our bodies were still close to one another as we continued kissing on the couch. His strong hands held me as his penis slipped out of me. Trying to get off of him, he persisted in his embrace, holding me so that couldn't get up.

"Not so fast," he said. I could feel his heart beating. "I just want to feel you for a little while."

My head was spinning. *Feel me for a little while? Why on earth did he want to do that?* I thought. It was usually more like 'okay, get up. We're done now'. I laid my head down on his chest. I listened to the beating of his heart as his hand stroked my hair. He gave the top of my forehead a tender kiss.

"There now, isn't that better?" he asked.

"Yes," I sighed. Inside, I was worried about what all of this meant. I hadn't intended to get caught up in a whirlwind of passion with Stark, but the way he looked at me made it unbearable. I just had to have a taste. I knew I would return to Blane soon and there was still a permanence of love left for him. Did this mean Stark loved me or was this simply another one of his conquests?

"You smell good. I love feeling this close to you," he said. His large hand continued to stroke the back of my head. His gentle embrace was so comforting.

"You do?" I said looking up at him.

"Yea, of course I do. You're amazing. What guy wouldn't want to make mad passionate love to you and then hold you afterward?" he asked.

"A lot," I responded. "Anyway, you don't really seem like the type for this sort of thing."

"What do you mean?" he asked.

"You know the whole hearts and cuddles thing. It doesn't seem like your cup of tea considering you're non-committal and all that," I said.

"So, this didn't mean anything to you just now?" he asked. He sat me up and looked at me with a puzzling expression.

"I mean....We had sex and I liked it," I responded. Stark sat up. I slid off of him and sat up next to him.

"It wasn't just sex for me Liza. Don't get me wrong, I've been wanting to jump your bones since you bashed me over the head and stole my row boat, but I like you," he said. I'm not really sure I believed him. *Why was he saying this to me?*

"I, um...I don't know what to say," I said.

"Say? I guess I was hoping you'd say that you like me too," he responded.

"Yes... Of course I like you. That's not even a question is it? It's just that..." I started.

"Just that what?" he asked. I thought for a while. This would all be very hard for me express to him.

"It's just that I'm confused about my feelings for you," I said.

"Wow, ouch. Really? Confused? Is this about Blane?" he asked. I looked away from him.

"No," I lied.

"You're a really bad liar. It's cool I get it," he said standing up and putting his pants back on. He threw me the pieces of my bikini.

"I'm not lying. Are you mad?" I asked.

"Nah, it's cool," he said. "I told you I could have you if I wanted."

"Is that what this is about? A conquest?" I exclaimed.

"No, of course not, but you're obviously still hung up on Blane. So, I have to see this for what it is, two consenting adults having a little fun. That's all," he responded. I fumbled to get my bathing suit back on. This was the awkward aftermath I was used to.

"Well, I'll have you know that I don't give my body up all that easily. I feel something for you, but I'm confused about what it all means," I said. He put his hand up.

"Listen, it's fine. You don't have to explain. I'll get you back to lover-boy in no time and we can just forget any of this ever happened. Friends?" he said.

"Yes, okay. Friends," I said nodding my head.

"I'm sorry. I shouldn't have had sex with you. I should have stopped," he said.

"It's okay. I asked you not to stop," I said turning to look at him as I entered my bedroom door. "I'm going to change clothes now and when I get back, we can go through the portal okay?"

"Okay," he said sitting down on the couch, buttoning his shirt back up.

I entered my room, shutting the door behind me as I did so. Opening my closet doors, I picked out a long red cotton dress and slipped it over my body. I admired my reflection in my full-length mirror stroking the material downward with my hand. I ran my fingers through my hair in an attempt to rid my locks of the tangles. I could hear Stark in the other room talking on his cell phone. I pressed my ear up against the door to get a better listen of what he was saying.

"Baby, I'm just going away for a few days. Relax. I'll be back soon..... No, I'm not cheating you," he said.

Cheating? I thought he didn't have a girlfriend. My body began to tense with anger. I could feel my cheeks become hot an flushed. We just had this whole conversation about him liking me. That lying sack of shit. I continued to listen to his muffled voice through the door.

"No baby.....Please don't hang up.....Baby? Are you there? Shit!" he exclaimed.

I could hold it in no longer, my nerves were bursting with confrontation. I pushed the door open. My eyes were burning with anger.

"Who was that?" I asked.

"It was nobody. You look amazing," he said. His lips up-turned into a smirk.

"Don't change the subject. Was that your girlfriend?" I asked.

"I told you, I don't have a girlfriend. Were you listening to my phone conversation?" he asked.

"That's irrelevant," I responded.

"Well, actually, I think it's pretty relevant. Why do you care anyway?" he asked.

"Hmmm, I don't know maybe because we just had sex and you have a girlfriend who cares about you? How could you do that ? I thought you were different than that. Do you tell all these women you care about them just to have sex with them?"

I asked

"Of course not Liza. If you'll recall, I didn't tell you I cared about you until after we had sex," he said. I rolled my eyes.

"Well, I wasn't talking about myself. I can't believe you have a girlfriend," I said sitting down on the easy chair next to him.

"She's not my girlfriend Liza, okay?" he said.

"Why not? Why do you say that?" I asked.

"Because she's boring and uninteresting. She's just not girlfriend material."

"Is that so?"

"Yes, that's so. Now drop it, okay?"

"Okay, fine. It's dropped. I'm still mad at you though."

"Okay, well, there's not a lot I can do about that," he responded. As I sat there in the chair with my arms crossed, I looked away from him. "Are you ready to make that portal appear?"

"I will when I'm ready," I said.

"Okay, when will you be ready? Do we need to have a snack first or say or prayer or something?" he asked. I rolled my eyes again.

"No, of course not. I just don't know if it's a good idea that you go with me. You don't have to do this you know," I responded.

"I know, but I want to," he said placing his hand over mine. I looked down at it and couldn't help, but smile.

"Ah, see there. You're not mad at me," he said.

"You're right. I'm not. Let's go," I said motioning for him to come into my room.

"Liza, you animal. I don't think I could go for round two until I get a drink of water first," he teased.

"Shut up this isn't a round two invitation. The portal is in my closet," I said.

"Your closet? Okay...." he said following me.

"Sit down," I said motioning for him to set next to me on the bed. As he sat down close to me, I felt the small hairs of his legs tickling mine. The sensation was a sweet reminder of our closeness.

"I told you, no round two," he joked again.

"Stop, this is how it works," I said lying down. He lied down next to me, turning his head to face me. His green eyes sparkled as I stared back at him.

"Now what?" he whispered, grabbing my hand.

"Shhhhh," I hissed. He tightened his lips, trying not to up-turn the corners of them. We laid there silently, gazing at one another. I gave his hand a tight squeeze. The clench of anxiety lingered in my gut. I knew I would have to use his name.

"Blane, I know you're there."

The rumble of the floor shaking beneath us gave the bed a slight vibration.

"Is that it?" he asked. He sat up.

"Lay back down," I said pulling on his shoulder. "It will appear in my closet. Blane please. Open it. Open the portal."

Again the floor shook. My bedside lamp began to flicker on and off. Stark stood up and began to search the room. He pulled my closet doors open, revealing only a rack of clothes.

"Nothing is really happening Liza," he said. He peered at me, raising a single eyebrow.

"Close that. It will, just give it time. I really doubt he likes it that you're here with me," I said.

"Well, maybe I should sweeten the pot a bit," he said, closing the doors to my closet shut. "Blane, you son of a bitch, I'm here to give myself up to you. You can have her. She's all yours."

The words stung a little. I didn't like the idea that I was something to give. The ground trembled a bit more now making it uneasy for he and I to steady ourselves. Walking over to him, I fell over a few times. My legs wobbled beneath me. I outstretched my hands to grab onto his strong arms. He did his best to steady me as we shook. The sound of rushing water filled our ears.

"Go ahead," I said. "Open the doors now."

I had a tight grasp on his arm as he managed to pry the doors open, revealing the rocky ledge. The cool mist of the falling water grazed our skin.

"Let's jump on three Liza," he said. "One, two..."

He leapt out into the water without allowing the number three to pass his lips, carrying me away with him. Down we fell into the black abyss, covered by the sensation of bubbles on our skin. I dared not leave the security of his arm as I held on tighter than before. The muscles in his arms constricted as if to tell me everything was going to be alright. Down, down, down we fell until the softness of the warm sand could be felt beneath our limp bodies. As my eyes adjusted to the sunshine overhead, I looked over to see if my friend had made safe passage to the island as well. Stark sat up, shaking his blonde hair about as he did so. The grit of the sand slapped against my skin.

"I guess we made it," he said.

"You didn't say three," I responded.

CHAPTER 9

MAKE A WISH

The branches in the trees were swaying about in the wind, clapping together like the sound of applause. It's as if they knew we were there to liberate the lost souls of Blane's island. The warm sand beneath us cradled our bodies while we became oriented with his world once again. I could feel the warm and fuzzy feelings, tingling throughout me ,masking all my fear and doubt. Although this beach wasn't familiar, I felt a false sense of security. I couldn't hear the sweet music of the village as I had before. The wind continued to carry with it the sounds of approval as the colorful birds overhead chirped at us.

"Where are we?" I asked.

"We're on Sedania, of course. Where else would we be?" he responded.   "I know we're on Sedania, but which part of Sedania? I don't recognize this beach," I said.

"We can't be far from him," he responded.

"Let's go then. We don't have time to waste," I said.

I stood up, feeling the warm sand beneath my feet. I could see the foliage of the forest not too far from us. I knew we would have to journey through it.

"Wait, where you going?" he asked.

"To find Blane," I said.

"What's your plan? Just walk into the forest? It's dangerous out there. I would know," he said.

"Do you have a better idea?"

"Yes, I say we set up camp for the night. In the morning we can build a raft to float us around the island without crossing the boundary. That way, we can get a better idea of where we are. We can find the village more easily that way," he said.

"What about Serena or the other mermaids?" I asked.

"You leave that to me. I know what I'm doing. Nobody will bother us as long as we don't cross the boundary," he said.

"Okay, fine, what do you need me to get?" I asked.

"Nothing," he said.

"Nothing? Really? We set up camp with nothing?" I asked.

"Liza, this is an island of dreams. How do you suppose I survived in the cove before? The fairies helped me. They helped you too. You just didn't notice. They come out when it's dark. We'll just have to wait for the sun to set," he said.

"Okay, you're the boss," I said. I sighed, resting my bum back down in the warm sand. The ocean breeze against my face was healing. I know I still had a frown though.

"Well, don't look so glum. There's plenty for us to do until then," he said.

"Oh really? Like what?" I asked.

"Come on, I'll show you," he said pulling my arm.

The cool ocean water came over my bare feet. He pulled me toward the dancing waves.

"Stark, what are you doing? No, I don't want to swim," I resisted.

"Come on Liza. Don't be that way," he said.

He drug me over to the edge of the water where the waves

could collapse over our feet just a bit and retract back into the ocean again. Taking both of my hands in his, he pulled me into the water while I resisted. Planting my feet in the sand, I refused to go any further with the water only rising to my ankles. He tugged on me, trying to coerce me further, but I was steadfast.

"Come on baby. Don't do me that way," he said.

I managed to wriggle free of his hands, turning on my heels and running in the opposite direction. Following close behind me, he ran after me. I darted in one direction to fake him out, then moved in the other, but he was on my tail like white on rice. Closing in on me, he wrapped his big arms around my waist, lifting me up off my feet. I squealed out loud as in his arms, I was suspended in the air. I kicked my feet, trying to free myself, but it wasn't advantageous. He swung me around his body as if I were as light as a feather, lifting me up and slinging me over his shoulder. I could see his feet walking me over to the ocean water.

"Okay, truce. I give up! Not in my sundress though," I protested.

He put me back down on my feet. The silliness slowed as we caught each other in a gaze of passion. I reached down to the bottom of my dress, pulling it up to my thighs. His hands grazed my skin as he helped me slide it up over my head. I could see the pleasure in his expression as he relished the sweetness of my skin. I stood there in my black bra and lace cheekie panties looking up at him. His fingers fumbled as he unbuttoned his shirt. I put my hands on his chest, feeling his smooth skin and muscles. He pulled off his pants and threw them to dry on the beach. In only his boxer-briefs now, I could see his member chubbing up with excitement at the sight of my half-naked body. I didn't want to allow this moment to go any further sexually, but I feared I may have triggered something in him. He pushed my silky brown hair out of my eyes as he angled my face toward him. He licked his plump lips and he moved his face in toward mine. I turned, only allowing him to kiss my cheek. It wasn't as if I wanted to deny him of my affection, but I couldn't indulge him either. I turned from his embrace as I went deeper into the water. The cool, wet feeling sent goosebumps all over my skin. I could see his disappointment. Raising up my pointer finger, I gestured for him to join me. The corners of his lips turned up, concealing his disapproval. He followed though. The waves moved us up and down in the water like fishing bobbers, pushing us further forward to the shore. Together we resisted the push, hooking arms and jumping with the waves each time they went upward.

"See now, that wasn't so hard. Was it?" he said.

"I guess not," I sighed tilting my head back to wet it in the water. He turned to face me, holding on to both of my arms this time.

"God, you're beautiful Liza," he blurted out.

"Why are you saying that to me?" I questioned.

"I'm sorry. I can't help it. Why wont you let me kiss you again?" he asked.

"Because. You know why. We're just friends remember?" I said.

"Friends don't have sex," he retorted.

"That was a mistake. I do love Blane, you know," I said.

"Well, if I remember correctly, you told me you loved me also," he responded. I gasped.

"But you were dead. How can you remember that if you were dead?" I asked.

"You know Liza, some say consciousness can exist outside the body. I can attest that is true," he shrugged. "I know you say you love Blane, but I've seen the way you look at me. I felt the way you made love to me."

"Are we going to swim or something or just stand here and talk about my feelings?" I asked.

"It's fine. Never mind. Forget I even said anything at all," he said.

"Done," I said jumping with the ocean tide. I yelled out in delight as the wave carried my body to shore. Stark's head perked up. It was no secret that he couldn't resist fun and games. He too thrust his body into the waves, moving to the shore in the tide. He looked at me nodding his head.

"Again," he said pulling me back into the ocean. Again we hooked arms, jumping up with the waves and pushing against the pressuring water. The sky was painted with pink and purple splashes of color as the sun was setting. Again, we plunged into the waves, allowing them to throw our bodies to the shore. We giggled as we tumbled about in the sand together. The body surfing in the waves continued for quite some time, sending us into a fit of joy. The sky was growing darker with each ride of the wave, but we didn't trouble with that. Blane's island had the gift of enchanting souls with their dreams in order to pry them away from the reality of life. It seemed perhaps that Stark and I had found a dream in one another where only the simple things mattered. With only our bodies and the strength of the ocean, we found cause to delight in our experience.

As we set foot out into the ocean again, the moon was beginning to rise on the horizon. It was full, round, and certainly much larger than I had ever seen before. Its stunning appearance shimmered in its reflection on the ocean water. The sky grew dark as thousands of twinkling stars dazzled brilliantly in the night's sky. Stark was getting into position to ride the waves again, when I placed my palm on his rock hard belly. Feeling the firmness of his muscles on my skin, filled me with a hopeful desire. I had hoped he would cross my friend-boundary. It was if I had painted a piece of cardboard to look like bricks. All he would have to do is take a closer look and see that he can take it down with one bare hand. It was a flimsy wall that only the slightest of convincing could break down. I stopped him, wanting him to see the beauty of our surroundings, but doing so awakened my eroticism.

"Look, isn't it beautiful?" I asked

"Yes, it's probably my favorite thing about Sedania. We better get to shore and put our clothes back on. The fairies will be out soon," he responded, taking my hand in his.

"Alright," I said. My voice was soft and submissive.

He grabbed up my red dress in his fist, handing it to me. I hesitantly pulled it up over my head, hoping he would come to ravage me. I paused as he pulled his jeans up over his buttock. With his back turned to me, I couldn't see if he were aroused by me or not. I wanted to take a step forward and fling my arms smooth around his belly, but I dared not make the first move. It was in his aggressive, animal behavior that I found myself most entrenched in lust. I wanted him to read my mind and know that he just needed to take a closer look at the faux brick wall. As he buttoned up his shirt and sat down in the dry, sandy part of the beach, I could see that he was taking my friendship request seriously. I straightened up my posture as if in doing so would make him believe that I were more conservative in my regard toward him. I sat down beside him, making sure I gave us each enough space. I extended my arms out, propping myself up from behind and extending out my fingertips to where they could almost meet his. Both us of were looking up, admiring the night's sky.

"I wonder what else is out there," Stark said.

"What do you mean?" I asked.

"You know like other planets, other beings, or deities. Do you ever wonder about things like that?" he asked.

"Not until recently. I never really believed in God. I remember going into church as a kid with my little bible, holding my mom's hand as the elders patted my head. I would always find the same old man who smelled like pipe tobacco. The truth is, I just loved the way his wool blazer smelled. Anyway, I remember sitting in church and thinking this is all bullshit. I have to try to be good even though I was born to be bad. That's not really fair, I thought," I responded.

"There has to be something out there bigger than us Liza. Just look at us here in another galaxy, looking back at billions of stars that could have their own civilizations. We've discovered a black hole that can be accessed in our sleep. It really is amazing when you think about it," he said.

"Oh yea? How do you know we aren't just dreaming? What if we really never did wake up?" I asked.

"It's not possible. If feels too real," he said.

"Yea well, my boobs feel real too. Don't they? It doesn't mean they are," I snapped.

"Actually, I can tell they're fake," he teased.

"Shut up! That was just an example! This is all me!" I retorted.

"Yes," he laughed. "I know. I'm just giving you a hard time."

He nudged my arm, throwing me off balance as my outstretched arms were still the only thing propping me up. As I fell down, I took a fist-full of sand in my hands throwing it back at him. We wrestled for a moment, but his strength easily out did me. He pinned me on ground with both of my arms up over my head. His grip on my wrists was loose and gentle however, allowing me to easily free my hands. I looked up at him placing my hand on his cheek, then running my fingers through his hair. I could feel his heart beat, pulsing on my chest as we caught our breath. He was looking at me with romantic eyes, capturing me in his allure. I took a deep breath, rolling my head back as if to fully indulge in the taste of his touch.

"We can't do this," I whispered.

"Do what? We aren't doing anything," He said rising up off of me. "You're just a cock tease anyway."

"I beg your pardon?" I said.

"You heard me. You dangle the carrot in my face, then tell me the two of us are only friends," he responded.

"I'm sorry. I just got carried away. I won't do it anymore," I said.

"Yeah well what's all this 'not in my sundress' and 'let's get half naked to swim in the ocean' shit followed by wrestling on the beach?" he responded.

"You instigate a lot of this stuff, you know?" I said.

"Yea I guess you're right. Look," he said pointing off into the distance where a small blue dot could be seen hovering around in the air. "They're here. They've found me."

He was grinning ear-to-ear, quite pleased with this discovery. He pressed his finger to his lips, reminding me to stay quiet as if not to scare them off. Soon many dots of color illuminated the air surrounding us as each fairy hovered about bearing a different shade of each color in the rainbow. Their feet landing on my skin felt like a pleasant little tickle. They would land momentarily and hover up over us again. Stark closed my eyes with his fingers and grabbed both of my hands.

"Now wish for something to appear," he whispered. I closed my eyes, taking a deep breath. I couldn't think of anything I wanted more than a glass of wine. I opened my eyes only slightly to find one sitting there on a rock.

"Extraordinary," I said out loud. The fairies blackened, disappearing from our sight.

"Shhhh," he hissed at me. We waited for a few moments only for them to reignite their brilliance upon our silence. "Wish for something else. They'll help us to set up camp."

"Why don't we just wish to be transported to the village?" I whispered.

"The fairies only help you enough to get you equipped to help yourself," he whispered back.

"Of course. How did that wine help?" I asked

"They realize your need to calm down," he whispered.

I kicked him, watching him grimace and trying to keep quiet. I again closed my eyes and imagined us in a beautiful fire-lit campground with a large canvas tent and chairs to make it more quaint. As I opened them again, I could see the things I imagined were forming around me.

"You're doing it," he whispered. I looked up at him and smiled at how proud I was of myself for imagining it. I pulled his hand to have him sit next to me by the fire. The fairies had been kind enough to leave us some additional wine with two glasses. They faded away into the distance as my wish had manifested. I felt it safe to raise my voice again to a normal level.

"Cheers," I said raising my eyebrows and clinking my glass with his.

"I gotta hand it to you kiddo. You're much better at the magical aspect of this island than I am. It took me a week to figure out why those damn fairies were bothering me. I would swat them away from me like flies and sleep in the sand by myself before I figured it out," he laughed.

"You would. It seems like the theme of your life," I teased.

"What do you mean?" he asked.

"I mean it seems like you would be the type to reject someone who wanted to give you a good thing. Like avoiding a meaningful relationship for example. You woo women into bed only to leave them when you find greener grass," I said.

"That's not true Liza. I just haven't found anyone who I really want to love," he responded.

"You can reword what I just said if you want, but in my experience if it looks and quacks like a duck, that's what it is," I said.

"You don't know me at all," he growled. "Don't tell me what I am."

I was taken aback by his obvious display of disapproval by what I had said. Perhaps I had been hasty in the manner in which I labeled him, but he himself told me he doesn't commit to a woman. This alone was enough of an inclination not to get caught up in a romance even though a big part of me deeply wanted to. I knew his kind well because this was the kind of man I acquainted myself with; always reaching for the unobtainable heart.

"I'm sorry, I didn't mean to upset you. I guess I should keep my thoughts to myself," I said.

"Yes, perhaps you should," he snapped at me, rising up from his place and retiring to our new canvas tent.

I let him go on his own accord, resisting the temptation to go after him. I knew I had struck a nerve. Looking up at the dazzling sky, I was reminded of the last time I was in Sedania with Blane looking up at the stars. He had always indulged me in such extravagance. I wanted so badly to look upon him again and straighten this whole thing out. I wasn't really sure how a relationship between us would work with us living in two different worlds, but it didn't stop me from imagining the possibilities. The catch was, of course, that I had to give up everything, including my memories, but I felt I could change him. That was me though; the eternal optimist. I always thought I could change a man's mind with my charms.

Stark's behavior made it clear that he would never change for a woman. I admired that kind of strength and wished it was something that I had. I always wanted the mind of man with the grace and beauty of a woman. A man could easily get over disagreements, never get emotionally attached following sex, and mastered the "I don't give a fuck" mantra like a champ. If only I could replicate Stark's attitude and walk around in my own body. I would conquer the world. No such luck was going to bestow itself upon me anytime soon however. I got up to go inside the tent for sleep. Stark was curled up in a large assortment of blankets and pillows, fast asleep. I stroked the top of his head before planting a kiss on it.

"Goodnight," I whispered, curling up next to him. I spooned him from behind placing my arm around his large chest. The weight of my body against his was just enough to keep us both pleasantly warm. He seemed to pull me in for a cuddle as I fell asleep next to him.

CHAPTER 10

OUT TO SEA

The sun peeked in through the canvas tent at me the next morning, awakening me from my sleep. The crackling of the fire was audible as the aroma of cooking fish passed through my nose. Wrapped up in a sea of soft squishy blankets and pillows, I hardly noticed that Stark wasn't there. I reached over to grab a large lump of blankets that I thought was his body lying there, but of course he was already busy making headway on our plan from the outside of the tent. I squeezed through the canvas flap that made a door, squinting as the sunlight hit my face. There was a large stick with fish on it cooking on an open campfire. I raised my hand over my eyes to shield them from the gleaming sun as I looked up out into the distance to find that Stark was working on our raft. When I caught his eye, I began waving like a little school girl with a crush.

"Good morning," he said. "Nice of you to join me. Would you take the fish off the fire? I think they're ready."

This was not the kind of breakfast I was accustomed to in Sedania. He certainly didn't have the resources to lavish me as Blane had, but I supposed it would have to do. It was almost sexy watching him take care of us even though we were roughing it. I picked the stick up off the fire and carefully placed it on a nearby rock. The dead fish were looking at me with their creepy eyes, convincing me that they were judging me for wanting to eat them.

"I generally don't eat things that still have their faces," I responded.

"Well, I'm sorry princess. You can eat the fish or starve," he said walking over to me and sitting down. He picked up the stick and began to pull back the scales of the fish, exposing the meat inside and picking out bites to eat. "It's not that bad."

Pulling back the scales of the second fish, he pulled out a large chunk of meat in between his index finger and thumb, extending it out in my direction.

"Here, eat. You'll need your strength," he said.

My stomach rumbled out loud as I put my hand over it. As I pressed my palm into my belly, I had hoped it would quiet. Looking down at the meat in his hand, my mouth salivated, telling me that I was hungry. I put my hesitant palm out underneath to catch it. Winking at me, he dropped it down. I closed my eyes to block out what I was about to do. I imagined a large feast of dark turkey, macaroni and cheese, and garlic mashed potatoes as I popped the small piece of fish meat in my mouth. The texture of the fish on my tongue morphed into a delightful array of flavors. I could taste the juicy dark meat turkey in my mouth, bursting with the bold flavor only my grandfather could perfect with his all-day smoking. The buttery smooth taste of the macaroni followed; sending my taste-buds into a happy frenzy. Finally, the garlic mashed potatoes, whipped up to a perfect consistency found their way into my hungry belly.

"God, that's delicious!" I exclaimed, grabbing the fish off his stick and pulling it apart to eat it.

"Well, well, someone is a hungry girl. I told you it's not bad didn't I?" he said.

"Yes, but you didn't tell me it could be anything I wanted it to be!" I said with a mouth-full of food.

"What do you mean?" he asked.

"You mean you don't know?" I retorted.

"Liza, don't talk with your mouth full. For God's sake take a breath," he responded. I swallowed hard, allowing the last bit of garlic mashed potatoes to settle down inside of me.

"It tastes like my grandparents Thanksgiving dinner. No lie. It's so damn good," I said beginning to sink my teeth into the fish again.

"Oh you smart girl you. I didn't even think to try that," he said, closing his eyes as if to imagine his favorite food. "There's nothing like mom's cheese enchiladas."

"You mean you've been eating burned fish this whole time?" I laughed.

"Hey, don't make fun. I've shown you a lot of things too," he said.

"I know you're right. When should we set out on the raft?" I asked.

"Soon. I've just about got them tied together," he said.

"Do you need help?" I asked looking at him sideways.

"No, of course not," he said with his pride showing.

"Don't be like that Stark. I can help you. I'm not helpless you know?" I said.

"Yeah I know," he said looking down. "You sure are beautiful though."

"Stop it," I said blushing and pushing on his arm. He flexed it to resist me, but in doing so announced his muscles like a town crier. He always managed to tease me into sexual frustration with the slightest of behaviors. My hand wanted to linger there, but I dared not make the same mistake again. I could feel myself growing wet as I flung my hair to the side and ran one finger down my own neck. Beads of sweat were beginning to trickle down his face and arms, making each crease of his muscles glint in the morning sun. We had barely begun our journey and already I was finding trouble in trying to control my urges.

"No," he said looking at me sincerely. "It's true. You're so beautiful."

He took his finger, running it up and down my arm and shoulder. I closed my eyes to relish his touch. His strokes moved down to my leg rubbing to my knee, then up my thigh.

"Why do you do that?" I whispered.

"Do what?" he asked. There was an innocence in his voice, but I knew it was not an innocent question.

"Turn me on. Why do you turn me on?" I asked looking at him straight in his beautiful face.   He grabbed a fist-full of my hair, pulling me into him for a wet lip lock. I tried to push him away with my palms pressed firmly on his chest, but it was impossible. The taste of his tongue on mine sent shivers down me as I pressed against him and then wrapped my arms around his body. Pulling me in by the waist, he forced me on top of him as he lay in the sand. I could feel him bulging out through his shorts, greeting my clitoris with a treat as I straddled him.

"No, we can't," I said.

"Just for a second Liza. I just want to feel of you," he said, pulling me back down for an entrenching kiss. It was difficult not to surrender to his advances, but I felt torn. How could I have sex with Stark on Blane's territory? It seemed earth shattering. He began to pull my dress off of me while I pretended to resist.

"Come on baby. Just for a second," he said.

"We can't," I said kissing him. "We have to stop. We have to get out on the raft."

"We will babe. We will. Don't worry," he said with the heavy breath of desire.

Suddenly, I began to feel the acid in my stomach churning like a cake mixer. The fish, although delicious, hadn't agreed with me. I began kissing him again, only pausing to shift my gut. I thought perhaps I could calm the storm by pushing it out of the forefront of my mind. The forceful nausea overtook me however, causing me to stop my sexual frenzy. My face turned pale as I clenched the front of my torso.

"What's the matter?" he asked.

"Nothing," I said.

"Liza, you're turning pale. What's wrong sweetheart?" he asked.

I lunged over to the side, removing my body from him as I hurled the half-digested fish into the sand. The hardness in his pants turned as limp as a spaghetti noodle.

"Well, that was a buzz kill," he said standing up. "I guess the fish wasn't good after all?"

"Yeah, I guess so," I giggled. "This is so embarrassing."

"Don't sweat it. We ought to get going anyway," he said making his way over to the raft to continue tying it down. I followed behind him.

"Let me help you Stark," I said kneeling down by him again, yet still feeling a bit queasy.

"You better let me handle it. You're not feeling well," he said. I pushed my way next to him, beginning to tie the raft together. "Stop it you're doing it wrong."

"Then, show me," I insisted. He sighed out loud.

"Look, you have to knot it twice or this bamboo wont stay

together," he said showing me how to knot the rope.

"Why didn't the fairies just leave you a row boat like they did before?" I asked.

"Actually that was a present from Blane," he said.

"Why did Blane give you a row boat?" I asked. He shrugged.

"You got me. It sure did the trick to get your attention though," he winked.

"You think Blane gave you a boat to get my attention?" I asked.

"No, of course not. That's the last thing he wanted. There now. Viola," he said admiring his work on the raft. "Do you think your stomach can handle a little choppy water?"

I nodded, assisting him picking up the bamboo raft. We placed it in the shallow part of the water, wading around. As we pushed the raft out, he looked over to me in reassurance.

"It's going to be okay Liza. She'll wake up," he said.

We mounted the raft, pushing through the waves and moving up and down in the water. The movement was turning my stomach, but I did not allow myself to vomit again. I suppose it was the morning sickness causing me to me feel bad, but I dared not let the news out to Stark. I wasn't really sure how he'd feel knowing he'd had sex with an already pregnant woman, but I had been swept away in the moment. We paddled out in the water on our bellies, drawing closer to the boundary. The idea that we may be ulimiliac food was not pleasing, but I pressed on, paddling around the island.

"What are we looking for?" I asked.

"Signs of civilization," he said. "We're here, we just got spit out on the wrong side of the island."

"Why don't we just ask Issiryth for help. She seems kind," I said.

"No, I don't trust her at all. If she's Blane's mother, there must be something wrong with her," he responded.

"Okay," I shrugged resuming the paddling when out in the distance I could make out the shadow of a ship drifting in the sea. It carried itself gloomily across the water like a ghost. I shuddered at the thought of it nearing us, but Stark pressed on with confidence.

"A ship," he said. "I've never seen a ship on Sedania. Maybe they can help us."

"Help us? Are you crazy? Why would they help us? We don't know anything about them. They could be dangerous," I said.

"Yes, true, but we are on this little raft and they have a big ship. They can probably take us to Blane," he responded, paddling in their general direction.

"No, Stark. Let's go back to the island. I have a bad feeling about this," I urged.

"Will you calm down? I've got this," he responded.

The ship drew closer to us. No longer just a shadow I could make out with large white sails and a big black cannon resting at the top of it. They flew a pirate's flag with a skull and cross bones. A man with white hair peered down at us with his binoculars yelling to the crew.

"Man overboard!" he said.

They had spotted us and in doing so, we were vulnerable and exposed to the dangers that may present themselves. Stark was still comfortable in his decision to pursue them, waving and encouraging them to rescue us. It was apparent he second-guessed his decision to set out to sea to find the village rather than venturing into the forest. I supposed both options were treacherous journeys, but boarding a pirate ship certainly did seem like the safer option.

"Let's turn around and go back," I said.

"Not a chance. Everyone on Sedania is in a happy trance. It's just some guy living out his pirate dream. It will be fine, I promise," he said.

"I don't like this Stark. Please there has to be another way," I urged.

"That's enough now princess. I wont let anyone hurt you," he said.

I could see them lowering a smaller boat out of the large ship with two men inside. They put their oars out to row toward us. They were all dressed up in red do-rags and tattered white shirts.

"Ahoy there!" the man said waving. Stark waved back, but I grabbed his hand to stop him, looking back at the pirate with a look of terrified disgust. "What's the matter little lady?"

"We're doing just fine. Y'all just go on back to your ship," I said.

"Oh, isn't that cute?" said the other man. "She thinks she can navigate the waters on her own."

"You know, you guys shouldn't be out here," said the first man.

"I know," said Stark. "But we just got here. We need to find our way to Blane's village."

"Is that so?" he said stroking his long, mangy red beard. "Well, you'll have to talk to the captain about that."

His large black and white grin led me to believe that we

wouldn't have the option to resist talking to the captain. Grabbing me by the arm, he forcefully pulled me into his rowboat as Stark voluntarily followed behind me.

"Don't touch her like that," he said.

"Or what?" said the red-bearded pirate holding up a large knife from the inside of his boot. Stark didn't respond and sat down next to me, squeezing my hand. I was frightened, but having him close to me made me feel a bit better. He had promised me, after all, that he wouldn't let anyone hurt me.

"Break it up you two," said the second pirate, sitting in between Stark and I. I quietly succumbed to his insistence as not to stir the pot.

The red-bearded pirate never took his eyes off of Stark as he smiled with his black teeth, showing us the knife as if to remind us that we were still under his rule. We rowed toward ship as I tormented over our predicament. How could Stark put us in such a scary situation? As we moved up to be flush with the ship, the pirates strung the rope through the pulley system. Little by little the rope pulled us up to the top. I could see Stark mouthing the words 'I'm sorry', but somehow that didn't quite cut it. I looked away from him, knowing that I was on my own. The pirates on the ship were in a frenzy over the sight of a woman, gawking and cat-calling me as the red-bearded pirate forced me onto the ship by my arm. I could see the other pirate detaining stark with the threat of a sword and tying his hands together.

"No!" I shouted. "No! Let him go."

"That's enough now love," he said pulling me through the crowd of shouting men. "The captain will see you now."

He then turned to address the men.

"That's enough now. The captain has an important meeting with a lady. Give him some privacy," he said pushing me through a small door in the back of the ship and shutting it behind me. I could see his face through a small window at the top of the door.

"No, please no. Let me go," I cried, trying to pry the door open, but it was no use. He was holding it closed.

"That's enough," I heard a deep, husky voice from behind me say. I turned around to behold the image of the captain who was holding me captive. "Why are you here Liza?"

I was shocked that he knew my name. I turned, looking at a tall man with black hair and a long, neatly groomed beard. His chocolate brown eyes had a twinkle as he winked at me. He was dressed a bit a more stylishly than his crew, wearing a neatly pressed white button-up shirt with black pants and boots. His teeth were straight and dazzling white as he smiled at me from behind his desk. He motioned for me to come have a seat with him as he poured two glasses of scotch on the rocks. I was terrified at the sight of him yet relieved he wasn't as detestable as his men. He was more refined in his demeanor. The way he shuffled across the floor as he walked commanded attention. There was something about his air that made me feel a bit more at ease although not all together comfortable as I approached him.

"Please have a seat," he said.

CHAPTER 11

THE KING

"What will you do to me? Are you going to rape me now?" I asked as I sat down in front of him.

"Why? Would you like for me to?" he asked with a devilish smile.

"No, of course not," I said ringing my hands together.

"There's no need to be nervous love. I'm not going to rape you unless you want me to, but then again is that even considered rape?" he laughed. His white teeth sparkled in his wide open mouth as he threw his head back.

"I don't know, sir," I said, cutting my eyes up at him.

"Your eyes are mesmerizing," he said clenching his own chest. "I can see why Blane fancies you."

"How do you know me? Can you get us over to Blane?" I asked.

"Well, that all depends. I'm a business man you know. I don't do something for nothing," he said.

"Okay, but you didn't tell me how you know who I am," I said.

"I know everything that crosses this sea. You ran into a mermaid named Serena if I recall. She is a feisty little bugger that one. It's too bad Blane exiled her to human form and took her as his prisoner. She was my favorite mermaid," he sighed.

"He did what?" I asked in amazement.

"Oh, you didn't know?" he said placing his hand over his mouth, "I've said too much. Forgive me Liza. Where are my manners? I'm Captain Butch Rylan. It's a pleasure to meet your acquaintance."

"Yes, the pleasure is all mine. What can you tell me about Blane? It's important that Stark and I get to him as soon as possible. He has my mother and we have to wake her up from a coma. The only way to do that is to get her and bring back over the boundary," I said.

"Hmmm," he said pressing his fingers to his lips. "I see your dilemma, but what's in it for me?"

I thought for a moment, looking off into the distance. There had to be something I could offer him, but what of any value could I give him?

"There has to be something," I sighed. "Is there something you want from Blane that you'd have trouble getting? Maybe I can get you something like that."

Butch thought for a minute, again pressing his finger to his lips. His elbow was propped up against the desk as he leaned in.

"Yes," he said. "I believe there is something Blane has that I want."

"Okay. What is it? I'll get it for you," I responded. I could feel the anxiety twisting inside of me.

"A lock of Issiryth's hair," he responded.

"A lock of Issiryth's hair? Why don't you just ask her for one? It seems like she has a lot of it," I said.

"I don't know if you've noticed, but nobody is allowed to go over the boundary. I've never been anywhere close to her since the islands split. I assume you have?" he asked.

"Yes, I've been to her island," I responded. Butch's eyes turned wide with astonishment at my proclamation.

"Well, well, aren't you quite the brave one? Well, I don't really care how you get it, but get it to me. He keeps it in a small black bag. I think he usually keeps it in his pocket, but not always. If you can get me some of her hair, then I'll help you on your mission," he said taking a large gulp of the scotch.

"Okay, one way or the other we will get it to you, but if we do, will you also take us back over to the boundary to return home once we're done?" I asked. I pushed my glass away (knowing a pregnant woman can't drink).

"With pleasure," he said grabbing a pen and paper from his desk.

"What are you doing?" I asked.

"I'm drawing up a contract and you're going to sign it," he said.

"Okay...no problem. What does it say?" I asked.

"It says that you agree to get me a lock of Issiryth's hair within three days. If you don't, then you and the gentleman have to join my crew and be my slaves forever," he responded.

"What? I can't agree to that! I have to get home to my children!" I protested.

"Then, don't fail Liza dear. It's really that simple. Do you want my help or not?" he asked. I nodded.

"Yes, Captain Butch. I want your help," I said grabbing up the pen from his hand and scratching my name on the bottom of the page.

"Good girl," he hissed through his prefect pearly, white smile, snatching up the paper and rolling it up. "Come get the girl!"

The red-bearded pirate emerged through the door abruptly, wrapping his large arms around me and and binding my hands together behind my back.

"What are you doing??! We had a a deal!" I exclaimed. Butch roared with evil laughter as the the pirate drug me out of his quarters kicking and screaming.

"That's enough now dear. Captain's had enough of you!" he said. I could see that we were approaching the piers of the island near the village. He had taken us there just as promised, but the manner of which I was being taken was entirely against my will. The island was covered with a mysterious darkness. A dark rain cloud that wouldn't shed any water loomed above it. I couldn't hear any joyful music nor were there any happy faces. In the distance, I could see a dark, black castle up by the mountainside. It's eerie appearance made me shudder.

"What happened? This doesn't look like Blane's village," I said.

"Shut up," he commanded.

Soon, another of the detestable pirates appeared with Stark who was also bound. We looked at one another with concern, although not saying a single word in fear of the consequences. What sort of mess had we gotten ourselves into? They pushed us out onto the pier, forcing us to walk in front of them. Butch was walking behind us with bowed shoulders and a dominant strut. There was not a soul at the pier, but only the sounds of the ocean waves and the abandoned buildings that were left standing. A chill in air blew threw us, sending us into an empty despair.

"Keep moving," he said as we moved closer to the old village that now more resembled an abandoned ghost town. I remembered standing in the street, mesmerized by a beautiful parade of colors and fine music. It was now a barren, sad place, holding nothing but old, crumbling buildings of chipped paint, broken windows, and half-burned structures. There were people lying down in the street dressed in rags, holding out their hands and asking for donations of gold to feed their families. Butch looked down at them in disgust, holding his head up high as he lead Stark and me through the village toward the castle.

"Where are we going?" I asked.

"That's enough," barked the red-bearded pirate pulling on the rope that was keeping my hands bound.

"I'm taking you to him," Butch said flicking the red-bearded pirate on the back of the head. "I didn't give you permission to speak. If you say another word, I'm going to bury you and lover boy in the ocean. Do you understand?"

"Yes," I whispered, looking down at my feet as they shuffled through the once happy village. The depressing scene around me led me to believe that something very dark had taken over Blane's island. This is not the world he had envisioned full of laughter and joy. The dark castle certainly hadn't been in the village before and didn't belong in a place that was created to be picturesque and charming. The people in the street sneered at us, bearing their teeth like rabid dogs as we passed them by. It was beyond disappointing that I couldn't grab a hold of Stark's hand, but it was comfort to know that he was close by. There were two guards dressed in black armor from head to toe await- ing our arrival at the gate of the castle. There was a disgusting swampy mote surrounding it's large opening.

"What's your business?" they asked Butch.

"I've got a gift for the King," he said gesturing at Stark and me. The guards looked us up and down, examining us for a mo- ment and then looked back at Butch.

"What would the King want with these two?" he asked.

"Oh, trust me. He has a particular interest in these two,"

Butch replied. They looked at one another frowning, then nodded their heads in agreement.

"Very well then. You have thirty minutes before we come in there after you," they growled, lowering the bridge to enter the castle.

"Thank you gentleman," Butch said clasping his hands together as if to say a prayer.

They pushed us across the bridge; each of us maintaining our silence. I could see Stark grimacing as they pushed him. It must have been difficult for him to lose control of the situation and he certainly owed me an apology for putting me in this position in the first place. He didn't strike me as the type who would apologize or admit wrong-doing easily, but I wouldn't hold it against him. Blane ruled here and we had to play his game whether we liked it or not. The courtyard was filled with people wearing black and white ballroom attire and dancing about to a rhythmic melody being played by a string quartet. Their ominous presence gave me a fright as they danced together. None showed their faces, however, as they were concealed by elaborate black and white masquerade masks. I could hear the sound of dull, evil laughter from beneath the masks as we walked through them to get to the main part of the castle. Even the pirates seemed unsettled by the ghost-like dance that was happening around us. More guards were standing at the doors, opening them up to us. There was a large room with high archways and a checkered black and white floor, filled with people dressed as if they had walked right out of the 1800's. We were instructed to stand in a line with the other impoverished people who had come to present to the King.

In the front of the room was a large red throne, shining like a beacon as a focal point for the people. A short man with gray hair entered, rising his hands to hush the crowd.

"All bow for his royal majesty," he said.

The room immediately heeded his instructions including the pirates themselves. Stark and I refused however knowing that his "majesty" was anything but. Dismayed by our obstinate behavior, Butch forced us each to bow down against our will. As his boots hit the floor and he entered the room, not a soul dared to utter a single word. Blane in all his glory entered wearing a king's crown upon his head as he sat on his throne. His hair was as jet black as I remembered and his black eyes cut down into the crowd with intensity. His face was just as adorable as it had always been. Although it seemed the black speck in his heart had grown considerably. He appeared to be truly evil.

"At ease," he said, allowing us all to stand up straight. The gray haired man pulled out a large scroll, announcing the first people to present their case.

"Levi Roberts," he said, gesturing for a poor old man to come forward.

The man was dressed in ragged clothes with a dirty face and bare feet. With him, he had a young woman who seemed no more than twenty years old. She had a cherry red face with long, wavy black hair. She wore a long white dress made of the finest linens. She was sobbing in the man's arms as he pulled her by the arm to present her to Blane.

"No Poppa. Please no," she pleaded to him, but he hushed her, instructing her to stand up straight and dry her tears.

"Go on man. I haven't got all day," Blane growled.

"Please sir," Mr. Roberts started. "Take my daughter. I want to give her a better life. She's hardworking, sings well, and she's a virgin."

"I see," Blane said stroking his chin. "What do you propose I do with her?"

"Whatever you'd like sir. I'll take whatever you're willing to offer. My wife and I are starving," he said.

"Very well, I suppose she will fit in well with the others. I'll give two silver," he said.

"No Poppa!" she exclaimed as the guards paid her father and took her away. "The others" I wondered what that meant. Did Blane keep many young, attractive women for his own sexual satisfaction? Who knew what he was capable of? The gray haired man approached the front of the crowd again.

"Butch Ryland," he announced. Butch and his pirates pulled Stark and me to the front of the crowd. I put my head all the way down to conceal my face with my hair. I was looking down at my feet, but could hear his gasp as he caught sight of Stark. Surely he would kill him. Before Butch could speak a word, Blane cut in with his angry, booming voice.

"Why have you brought me this man?" he said.

"I've brought you a woman too. Perhaps you can put her with the others," Butch said.

"Shut up Butch!" Blane growled. "This one will be put to death."

I raised my head to look at him, making direct eye contact. His jaw dropped, looking at me. He was standing there quite speechless as his eyes began to glaze over.

"No Blane! Don't kill him. You'll have to kill me first!" I exclaimed. The crowd spectated closely at what he might say next. It was quite certain nobody often challenged him in this way.

"Liza?" he whispered as tears slipped out of his eyes.

His feet quickened upon the ground as he ran up to me, clasping his hands gently behind my head. His black eyes peered down into my soul, touching my heart once again with the heat of his passion. He placed his hand on my face, kissing my forehead and holding me close to him as if we had never left each other's side.

"I thought I'd never see you again," he whispered, then looked over to Butch. "I'll give you whatever you want for her. Name your price."

Butch's eyes lit up as if he had hit the jackpot of all jackpots. Blane was literally offering him whatever he wanted. I had hoped he would simply ask for the lock of Issiryth's hair, but I feared perhaps it wasn't that easy.

"A thousand gold pieces," he announced.

"I'll give you two thousand gold for her, but I don't want the man. Take him, kill him, do what you will with him," he said.

"No Blane!" I pleaded. "Please no! You can't. He's my friend."

"You still love this man don't you Liza?" he sneered. "I loved you and gave you everything and yet you've come back to rub him in my face. Why don't you just let me be?"

"Blane, please. We can talk about this later okay?" I asked. The crowd was still watching us with all of their attention.

"I'll do anything for you," he said, then turned to address his guards. "Give the man what he wants."

"It was a pleasure doing business with you," Butch said as he collected the money.

The guards began to untie my ropes, freeing my hands, but I could see they weren't going to extend the same courtesy to Stark. I looked over at Butch.

"You received payment for me. Why did you ask me what you could get out of this? Obviously you got something anyway," I said.

"I'm a pirate Liza. I don't apologize for nothing. Three days," he said in a threatening way as he left with his other pirates. I ran over to Stark who was still tied up.

"Untie him," I said looking over at Blane. Blane wouldn't look at me because he knew what he was about to say would lead to my disapproval.

"Take him away," he said to his guards as they each took him by an arm.

"No, you can't!" I exclaimed.

"It's okay Liza," Stark said. "I'm going to be fine."

"No! They can't do this to you!" I exclaimed. Stark hung his head as he went in step with the guards. I turned to Blane.

"What are you going to do with him?" I asked.

"He broke the law Liza. He's going where all criminals go, to jail," he said.

"To jail? I broke the law too. Do you not remember that?" I asked.

"Queens don't go to jail. It may not be fair, but I can forgive you. I can't forgive him," he said, scooping me in by the small of back and leading me away. "I'm done Banks I'm not seeing anyone else today. Liza and I are retiring to my bed chambers and I don't want to be disturbed for the remainder of the day. Do you understand?"

The gray haired man turned to him.

"Yes sir," he said turning to the crowd. "You are all dismissed."

Disappointment filled the air as the other peasants gathered their things to leave. None the less, the bodies cleared the room. Blane led me up to a small staircase off the main room where the two of us couldn't be seen by anyone. We made it a few steps up before he pressed me up against the wall. His breath was heavy with desire. I could feel my heart pounding. He pressed his lips against mine, kissing me with the fire of passion. I never had the ability to easily resist him, but I had so many unanswered questions. I was beyond disappointed with the way he had handled things with Stark. I pressed my hands up against his chest as if to form a barrier between the two of us.

"What's the matter Liza?" he said. "Can't you see that I've missed you. I can't bear to be apart from you."

"Well, by the looks of it, you've been staying rather young. I'd say you're doing just fine without me," I said

"Don't be like that. Please, it's been difficult trying to manage without you. You're my greatest weakness. Surely you see that," he said.

"I don't know what I see Blane. I've come back for my mother," I said bluntly.

"I see," he said, looking down. His demeanor turned dark with disappointment. "So you haven't come back for me?"

"No, although I admit. I'm happy to see you again," I said touching his face.

"Do you love Stark?" he asked boldly.

"Yes," I whispered.

"How? How can you love him? I love you. I'd die for you Liza. Why can't you just choose me?" he said.

"I love you too Blane. I love you both in different ways. Can't I love you both?" I asked.

"It hurts me Liza, but I'll take it. I'll take any amount of pain to be with you. You're here with me now. That's all that matters anymore. Will you come to bed with me?" he asked.

His hands had a tight grasp around mine as I thought for a moment. It was odd being in a castle instead of his house on the mountain overlooking the beach. I wanted to resist him, but I found it hard to do. I had missed and longed for the touch of his skin upon mine. There were so many thoughts rushing through me. He loved me despite my love for another man, willing to fight for my heart. I held him close, begging the question in my own mind of whether or not I was ready to go down this road with him again. The rush of desire began to overtake my body. His black, soulless eyes peered into my broken heart. His cold, pale hands clasped inside of mine giving me the affirmation of his love.

"Yes," I said in a low, breathy voice. His arms tightened around my waist as he lifted me. He held me in his arms as he climbed the steps to a door that led to his bedroom. There was a large bed against the wall with four ornate wooden bed posts. The room had large windows that opened up to a picturesque view of the beach from a balcony. He swung the door shut behind him with his foot as he laid me down on the soft, red comforter. The bed swallowed me with plush luxury. He pushed his raven-black hair from his face as he looked down at me. His dark eyes pierced me with their eery, yet seductive glimmer.

"You're mine Liza," he said. I could feel the heaviness of his body as he leaned over me. He put his plump lips up to my earlobe. "And I'm not giving you up again."

CHAPTER 12
GIVING HIM THE NEWS

The weight of his body on top of me was familiar, yet a bit unwelcomed. I wasn't yet ready to succumb to his every desire. I wondered why his island was so desolate and gloomy or how he maintained a youthful appearance despite his unfulfilled wishes. I couldn't bear the thought of what they may do to Stark to punish him for his crimes. My stomach began to turn again as the nausea relapsed. I could feel my whole body attaining a wave of heat as I turned pale.

"What's the matter?" Blane asked.

I got up and jolted to the nearby window and pushed it open. I stepped out on the balcony where I doubled over the wrought iron railing. I projected more of the fish breakfast.

"Are you okay Liza?"

"Yes," I said wiping my mouth. "I guess I'm just a little sick."

"You poor thing. You've been through a lot just to get to me and look at me unable to keep my hands off of you. Don't worry. I'll get Leila," he said.

"No Blane," I pleaded. "Don't get her. She hates me."

"Nobody hates you Liza," Blane responded. "Just stay put."

Blane disappeared through a door, coming back promptly with a wet wash rag and some round white pebbles in his hand.

"Here," he said putting one of the pebbles in my mouth and wiping my forehead with the rag.   "This ought to help."

The pebble melted in my mouth like the wax of a candle, sending a sweet chill of peppermint throughout me. My stomach felt immediately at ease the moment the flavors touched my belly. I laid back on the pillow letting out a sigh of relief while Blane felt of my face and neck.

"You don't feel feverish. Maybe you ate something that didn't agree with you," he said.

"Yea, that's probably it," I responded sitting up. "Blane, I need you to tell me what's happened since I've been gone and where my mother is."

"I will, but would you like me to have Leila bring us something to eat first?" he asked.

"No, no more wine and dine Blane. I need to know," I said looking at him with my hand on his face. He put his hand on mine pressing it deeper into his skin.

"I'll tell you, but I'm afraid you'll hate me," he said.

"Why would I hate you? I could never hate you," I responded.

"Because of what I did to keep myself looking young for you Liza. I let down everyone, but I knew you would come back and I didn't want to be an old man when you did," he said.

"You were an old man when I met you and I still wanted to be with you anyway," I said.

"Liza," he said holding my hands in front of me. "I make them suffer so that I will be okay. That's why my island has fallen into disrepair. Everyone needs gold to buy food and goods, but I keep everything scarce and limited. I didn't care about anything when you left."

I pulled my hands away from his, looking at him with disgust.

"How could you? They trusted you. They thought you could offer them a good life here..." I started.

"And I can," he said. "I promise you I can. Now that you're here everything will go back to the way that it was."

"And what about my mother?" I asked. He looked away.

"She gone away Liza," he said.

"She what? Where in the hell is she? Tell me right now. I came here to get her," I said.

"She's on the island, but I'm not sure where. She said she had to find you. She left in the middle of the night and I never saw her again. I don't know where she is," he said.

"You really expect me to believe that? You're 'King!' This is your island! You know everything that happens here!" I exclaimed.

"I don't. I swear. I'm only half deity. The rest of me is human. Remember?" he persisted.

"Issiryth."

"What about mother?"

"She knows where she is. She knows all pertaining to Sedania. Does she not?" I asked.

"Yes, I suppose mother would know, but we're estranged. She hasn't offered me one shred of support since you left. She's made the boundary twice as hard to cross. Serena has been exiled to human form for treason. I took pity on her and let her work for me in the castle however," he said.

"I thought you turned her into a human," I responded.

"Who told you that?" he asked.

"Butch," I responded.

"I wouldn't trust a pirate if I were you. They're not known for being honest," he said.

"Yea, tell me about it," I said rolling my eyes.

"Liza, you didn't make any sort of deal with Butch did you? He's an evil man to his core. He would have brought you to me regardless you know," he said. His black eyes blinked as he looked back at me. I thought for a while, thinking it best I didn't admit to the contract I had signed.

"No, I didn't. Why would you bring that up?" I asked.

"Because making a deal with him is ironclad and he's known for making wagers. I wouldn't be able to save you from him. Promise me you didn't make a deal with him," he said.

"Well, didn't you make a deal with him when you exchanged gold for me?" I asked.

"That's different and you know it. Promise Liza. I can't stand the thought of losing you again," he said.

"No, I didn't," I said looking away as I always did when I told a lie.

"I hope you're telling me the truth," he said.

"I am. Now tell me how we are going to get my mother back. She's in a coma. I have to wake her up," I said.

"We will Liza. I just got you back. I don't want to lose you again," he said pulling me in close to him.

"Then do as I ask of you. No more games Blane. I love you, but you know our circumstances prevent us from being together. You have to understand that," I said.

"I understand nothing of the sort! It is only by my good graces that you woke up. If I hadn't taken you through the portal after the crash God knows what else may have gotten to you. I saved you. You may not see that now, but I did!" he exclaimed.

"You could have just taken me across the boundary and fed me to the ulmiliac so I would wake up. You knew how to send me back to my life and children, but you didn't. You wanted to keep me because you were selfish. You kept Stark too and all these people. Why did you do it?" I asked.

"You wouldn't understand," he said looking down.

"Try me," I rebutted.

"Don't press me Liza. I'm in no mood. Things could be a lot worse for you trust me," he said.

"Is that a threat?" I asked.

"No, it's not a threat. It's a promise! The stories of heaven and hell aren't all that far fetched you know? Except there's multiple Gods and Goddesses and multiple universes that live by their own set of rules. A soul can travel far beyond what can be imagined in your physical world. Some of them are bad. Really bad and any number of them could have reached out to grab you, but instead I did. Do you understand? Me. I was the one to reach and grab as many as I can. I don't care what my mother says," he looked at me with great intensity sitting there on the bed as if he expected me to reciprocate with some sort of answer, but instead I said nothing.

I blinked a few a times with my large brown eyes, just awaiting his next speech. I didn't know what to say, but there were several things looming in my mind. First, was my mother of course. Second, was remorse for signing Butch's contract. He wanted a lock of Issiryth's hair which apparently Blane kept in his pocket, but how would I attain it?

"Well, aren't you going to say something Liza?" he said looking back at me.

"What do you want me to say? Thanks for saving me? Perhaps I could have found something better. Something that didn't try to convince me that dying was a better option than waking up and taking care of my children. Maybe I wouldn't be back here looking for my mother. Issiryth would have never kept us like this Blane and you know it," I said.

Blane was silent looking back at me with his glazed over black eyes glaring. I could tell that my words had hurt him a great deal, but what could I say under the circumstances? He had taken away my option with half-truths so that he could have me for himself.

"Perhaps you're right Liza. I wont try to keep you anymore. You can go if you wish," he said defeated.

"I want my mother back Blane," I said.

"I know!" he growled. "I don't know where the fuck she is."

"That's fine then," I said standing up. "Where's my room?"

"This is your room unless you want to a cell next to your buddy Stark," he said.

"Anywhere is better than here with you!" I exclaimed.

"Fine then, you can pay for your crimes too!" he burst, turning toward the door and shouting down the hallway. "Guards, come and take her!"

"No!" I shouted. "Blane! No! I have to get mother!"

Blane turned away from me as for me not to see his tears. Two large men wearing black suits came in and forcefully put my hands behind my back, cuffing me.

"Please Blane! Don't do this! I love you! Please!" I shouted in a fit of tears, buckling my knees and dragging my feet. "Blane, please! Let me go!"

He turned around and looked at me, raising his hand to the men holding me captive. As he gestured for them to cease their activity, they stood me up on my feet to face him. Tears streamed down my face as he placed his finger up under my chin and pulled my face up to look at him.

"I love you too, but you're an ungrateful little bitch and you need to learn a lesson," he said.

"What's happened to you? You're so evil," I said sniffling.

"You happened. I never loved a woman the way I loved you and you rejected me," he said.

"Blane, I'll stay here with you. Please don't do this. Please baby," I said.

He looked down with crying eyes to face the floor beneath us. I could tell that my words were penetrating his emotion. I had spoken directly to his heart and he would trouble over punishing me. I knew that convincing him that I was on his side would be the only way I could free Stark or save my mother. So, again, I found myself in the position of having to pretend in order to be free of him. How could I love this man that I also so desperately despised? It was difficult to pinpoint my reasoning.

"Blane please," I pleaded as he gestured for the guards to drag me away again. "I'm pregnant! I'm pregnant!"

"Stop!" he shouted. The guards once again ceased their detainment. "What did you say?"

"I said I'm pregnant. I'm having a baby," I said.

He grabbed me by both of my shoulders, holding my face close to his as he spoke.

"Say it again," he whispered.

"I'm pregnant," I reiterated.

"Release her," he commanded. The guards did as he said, releasing my hands and looking to Blane for their next instruction. "Please leave us alone now!"

The guards looked a bit shocked by it all, but did as he said, shuffling out of the room.

"Liza," he said with tears bursting from his eyes and a shaky voice. "Tell me again. Tell me again."

"I'm pregnant Blane," I said.

"It all makes sense now. All of it. You couldn't have made the portal appear otherwise," he whispered.

"What do you mean?" I asked.

"Nobody can get in and out of the portal unless he or she is accompanied by a decedent of Issiryth. The baby brought you to me. I thought mother had done it," he said.

"No, Blane. I don't know if the baby is yours. I was with someone else before I met you. I thought you might have opened the portal," I said.

"No I didn't," he said excitedly. "Do you know what this means Liza? It means you broke the curse. I'm finally going to have the family I've always wanted."

"You're wrong Blane. The baby isn't yours," I said.

"Bite your tongue Liza. That baby is mine and I'll see to it that its taken care of. I'm so happy! You have no idea. I'm sorry I got angry with you," he said. He pulled me in for a loving embrace. His lips pressed against mine.

I suppose my initial reaction was to resist him, but I knew I mustn't. The only way to escape his wrath and fly under the radar was to manipulate his emotion towards me. Blane wanted nothing more than a baby with a woman who would truly love him. The cruel irony in this scenario,was the woman who truly loved him, also hated him. Despite our emotional and physical connection, it was apparent that he was truly evil, only chasing love for his own agenda. After the things he had burdened me with, I had grown to despise him, yet I loved him. I wanted him to die, yet I desired him so much. I'm certain he sensed my hesitation as he pulled me closer to him, kissing me with more passion each time I pulled back. The desire in his lips announced their intention to ravage each crevice of my body. It would be a lie to say that in the heat of this moment, I didn't want to be ravaged, but in his manner of distracting me, I found myself angered. How could he again put my family on the backburner while he chased his own dreams? Only a horrible, selfish person could do such a thing.

"Ask me to make love to you Liza," he said, biting my earlobe.

He was wearing me down again. I could feel the excitement between my legs at the thought of having him inside of me. The muscles of his chest pressed against mine as he grabbed my ass. I could feel my breath becoming heavy with desire as he took down the straps of my red dress and kissed my shoulders. The weakness in my knees, gave way to the wave of passion that was finding its way through my body. I lowered myself onto the bed as he continued to kiss my neck and shoulders. Quite swept away again, I held my tongue.

"Ask me Liza," he commanded again, pulling my dress from my body.

He kissed down in between my breast and on to my stomach. Then, pulled my panties down with his teeth. As they slid them down my legs, I raised up my hips to allow them to come down around my toes. I shivered with excitement following each touch of his hand across my skin. His lips pressed up against my feet, making their way to my thigh and circling around to tease my sex. I moaned out, wishing he would pleasure me.

"Please," I mustered as he continued to kiss around my thigh and belly.

"Please what?" he retorted.

I thought for a while. Although I was quite angry with him for wanting to make love to me, I also wanted it more than I could bear. I didn't want to allow myself to get sucked back into his insanity, but I knew that resistance was futile. So, I suppressed my anger with the mask of passion and gave way to his request.

"Make love to me Blane. Make love to me as you never have before," I said.

His hands ripped off my bra, exposing my bare naked breasts. Placing his hand around my entire breast his lips sealed around my nipple as his tongue danced over it. He quickly undressed himself, plunging his rock hard cock inside of my warm, wet pussy and rocking his hips back and forth inside of me. I wrapped my hands around the back of his head, intertwining my fingers in thick black locks of hair. Arching my back, I screamed out at the pleasure. His cock was hard and throbbing. I could feel his heartbeat pulsating on the walls of my vagina. I could feel myself growing wetter with each thrust.

"Oh Blane, don't stop!" I exclaimed, rocking my hips forward to allow him to penetrate me deeper.

"You're mine now Liza. Don't ever forget it," he said to me.

His thrusts became deeper and more violent with each movement until he was pounding me; hard. His eyes became inflamed with red, hot desire. My fingers intertwined in the blankets as I grabbed a fistful in each hand. I arched my back, letting out the scream of my passion. I worried I ought not become so animated. Would it hurt the child I was carrying?

"Blane, Blane! The baby," I said.

"Just for a minute," he said as he continued.

Moving in and out of me, he grunted like a pig. Beads of sweat were rolling down his face. He grimaced pumping like crazy. The moans of his climax echoed across the room. Completely out of breath, he rolled off and laid next to me. I turned my back to him as I rolled over, but I could feel his sweaty body curling up next to mine and pulling me in. I moisture of his sweat wet my back. I was disgusted by such a gesture. *Didn't he think of the baby at all?* I thought. Like a slimy snake, I felt his kisses on my back.

"What's the matter?" he asked, still panting.

"Nothing at all sweetheart," I lied. "Nothing at all."

CHAPTER 13
THE STORY OF US: HER HAIR

He interlaced his tiny fingers in her long golden locks as the sea breeze gently whisked through his raven hair. The waves crashed on the beach with their playful banter. In his three-year-old mind, there was no better place on earth than here on this warm day in his mother's arms. She put her boy up in her lap as they watched the waves rise and fall with the ocean tide. He was mesmerized by her perfect creamy white skin and the way her hair fell down over her shoulders and into his hands as he played with it. She hummed him a sweet lullaby with the soothing sound of her velveteen voice, playfully clapping his hands together to each word. It was a bond between a mother and son, which could seemingly never be broken. The sound of a man's voice could be heard in the distance like a deep thunder clap on a stormy night.

"Where's my Izzy?" he said.

A tall man with long brown hair and pearly white teeth beheld her as the most beautiful creature he had ever seen. Kneeling down before her, he offered her a single red rose as a token of his affection.   "Thank you my love," she giggled as he seated himself next to her in the sand.

"You know, the boy needs a father Izzy. You can't just raise him alone on this island," he said.

"I know that Butch. Don't you think I know that?" she said looking away to avoid eye contact with him. He placed his gentle hand upon her knee to show understanding. She rarely cried, but when she did, it was only out of sheer devastation. The raven-haired boy gently removed the tear from his mother's cheek as she sobbed.

"Don't cry mommy," he said as he kissed her. She held her boy close, looking over at Butch who was still touching her.

"He's right Izzy. You're much too pretty to cry," he said.

"I have to send you back in the morning Butch. I can't keep you here, not after what happened last time," she said.

"I won't turn evil like him. I love you and the boy too much. Please just let me stay," he pleaded.

Her blue eyes puddled up with tears once more as the boy brushed her hair with his fingers, pulling it to his face to feel of its softness on his skin. Her hair was enchanting for many reasons, but for the boy, it made him feel so much closer to her and that was reason enough for him to love it. Restless in his place in his mothers lap, he jolted up at the sight of a crab that walked sideways on the beach, chasing it into the water, then squealing with delight.

"He's so happy. Look at him. How will he feel when I'm gone?" Butch asked.

"Don't bring him up. You know he's my only weakness," she said.

He grabbed her hands looking into her eyes.

"And why can't I be your weakness? Just let me stay. I love you," he continued to plead.

"Stop, it's already been decided. I've taken many lovers since Blane's father passed and I can take many more. I've enjoyed being with you, but it's time for you to get back to your life. I promise I'll send you with blessings of fortune. You'll never want for anything again. Not even for me. It's the way it is.

It's the way I created things. Don't fight it," she said to him.

"But I will always long for you," he said.

"Not if you have no memory of me," she retorted. "Now let's enjoy our last evening together."

He held her close to him as they watched the boy play in the waves, screeching out loud each time they crashed against him. She worried that Butch was a bit short-sighted about how the fibers of the island can fester in the veins of a human. Their desires are never quite satisfied. There was no reason that he too would not succumb to his evil side after a time despite his insistence that he would never overindulge. Butch ran down to greet Blane who was every so playfully enjoying the simplicity of his surroundings. He grabbed his arms swinging him around in a circle as did so.

"Faster Butch!" he squealed as Butch gained speed, throwing the young boy over his shoulder. Issiryth couldn't help but smile, watching her boy interact with him in such a way. There's nothing that warms a woman's heart more so than to watch a man interact tenderly with her child. He landed him in the sand, tickling his toes. The boy giggled out loud, trying to squirm away only to show that he was enjoying the sport of it. They played together on the sandy beach, Issiryth watching each smile and banter. She knew the boy longed for human friends just as much as Butch longed to stay, but it was wrong of her to keep him. She likely should not have loved Blane's father enough to have a child with him in the first place, but it was a mistake she couldn't take back.

"Blane, it's time for bed now. Tell Butch good night," she said.

"Awe mom, no. I don't want to go to bed," he responded. Butch pulled the boy up to hold him, kissing him on his cheek.

"Do as your mother says Blane. I'll tell you a bedtime story," he said. The boy hugged his neck.

"Okay," he said as he skipped off toward the house that Issiryth had built for them. Butch put his arm around her, kissing her on the head as they walked behind the boy.

"He is going to miss you considerably," she said.

"Let's not talk about that now," he said. He turned to her. Her beautiful blue eyes shimmered in the rising moonlight. He gave her a gentle kiss as he pulled her slender body to his.

"Ewww. That's gross," said Blane.

"Come on you," Izzy giggled, taking the boy the hand.

Blane was snuggled in his bed, holding his favorite teddy bear and propped up with several big, fluffy pillows. Issiryth and Butch settled in on each side of him, each giving him kisses as Butch prepared his bedtime story. She tried to hold back her tears, knowing that this family picture would soon dissolve into oblivion. The boy put one arm on his mothers shoulder, gently stroking her hair as Butch spoke.

"Once upon a time, there a was a young man who more than anything wanted to find a chest filled with gold. It was hidden on a forbidden island off the mainland. The problem was, he was a farmer's son and he'd never been out to sea before. His father disapproved of him leaving..." he started.

"Why couldn't he leave?" Blane asked.

"Because his father wanted him to be a farmer like him and farmers don't go out to sea. So, one day the young man decided he would run away in the middle of the night and stow away on a pirate ship. He was finally going to have the adventure that he had always wanted. When he saw the big ship docked at the pier, he felt a little bit scared because he'd never been away from home before. He didn't know what the pirates would think of him or do to him, but he found his way onto the ship anyway through a small opening while the pirates were sleeping," Butch narrated.

"Then what happened?" asked Blane in wide-eyed wonderment.

"Well, he spent the night in the belly of the ship and woke up to the captain standing over him, prodding him with a stick asking him what he was doing there. He stood up quickly, staring the captain right in the face saying 'I'm here to serve you captain.' The captain looked at the boy who was all dressed up in his farmer clothes and asked him what on earth he would do with a boy like him. He thought for a while, pondering what he may be able to offer to a pirate. Pirates were businessmen, after all. The boy would have to repay him for his kindness. 'Please captain, let me stay. If I stay, I'll work as a part of your crew and help you find the treasure chest on the forbidden island.' The captain thought for a while, stroking his long black beard, then his eyes lit up as if he had an idea...." Butch stopped, stroking his own facial hair just as the captain would have. Blane was in awe in of his portrayal of the exciting character as he sat, actively listening.

"What did the captain say?" Blane asked with wide-eyed wonderment.

"He said: 'I've never had a son before and I wont be around forever. If you come with us you have to give up your family forever and call me dad. I'll raise you up to take my place as captain when I die. What do you say?' Well...the boy didn't know what to say. He loved his father and the idea of leaving him forever was a bit scary, but he wanted the golden treasure chest more than anything he had ever wanted before. So, with that, he nodded his head and the captain took him in. He spent the next few years learning to how to be a pirate. He could sword fight and command the crew just like his new dad, but he still hadn't been to the forbidden island. He had embarked on the journey when he was only a teenager, but now he was all grown-up. The captain had grown to love the boy with all of his heart and more than anything he just wanted the boy to be happy," Butch looked down at Blane as if he was speaking directly to him about their relationship.

With Issiryth's hair in one hand, and a fist-full of Butch's shoulder in his other, he looked back up at him with his large black eyes to see what he would say next.

"Did he get him the gold?" Blane asked.

"No," Blane's face turned to disappointment as Butch continued "His father grew very old, and very sick. One day the young man was feeding him his soup on his death bed, when he told the boy how to find the treasure chest and handed him a map. 'X marks the spot' he said as he took his final breath. The boy was sad that he lost his father, but what he left him with was even better. He had a whole legacy; a ship, a crew, and a plan to get the gold....."

"Did he ever find the gold?" Blane asked.

"Yes, he found it and sailed back to the mainland. When he got there, he went home to visit his old farm. His dad was a lot older and withered, but he couldn't have been happier to see him. He shared his gold with him and they lived happily ever after. The End," said Butch as Blane's eyes became heavy and tired.

"Butch?" Blane said in a quiet whisper.

"Yea?" he responded.

"Will you take me on a pirate adventure to get the gold?" he asked. Issiryth and Butch looked at each other and smiled, but it wasn't only because the question itself was precious. It was a smile that bears the harsh undertone of pain, knowing that Butch and Blane would never see each other again.

"Of course. When you're a bit older we'll go," he said.

Blane held tight to a fistful of Issiryth's hair as Butch got up and kissed him on the forehead as he left the room.

"Goodnight buddy. I'll see you in the morning bright. Meet me on the beach?" he said looking at Issiryth.

"Yes, just let me get him tucked in," she said. Butch left the room and shut the door behind him. He still had it cracked slightly however, listening to what Issiryth was saying to him. Her voice was like an angel as she sang to him sweet lullabies.

"Mommy, stay with me. I'm scared. I don't want to sleep alone," he said.

"You sleep alone almost every night my love. What's wrong?" she asked.

"I just miss you and Butch when you're not with me," he said stroking her golden hair.

Issiryth got up, making her way over to the dresser and pulling out a pair of sheers. Looking in the mirror, she tied a ribbon around a lock of her hair, tying it in a neat bow, then cutting it off.

"Mommy, what are you doing?" he asked in astonishment.

"I'm giving you a very special gift," she said holding it up, then pulling a small black bag out of her pocket and placing the hair inside. She synched the bag up and put it in his tiny hand. "Here, I want you to have it."

His eyes were wide with amazement at the special gift, holding it close to his heart.

"Thank you mommy," he said.

"Now this is very special Blane. This is the most valuable thing that anyone could ever want," she said. Butch pressed his ear against the door. He couldn't imagine what she meant by that.

"My hair has magic in it and anyone who possesses some of it, will also have magic," she said.

"I have magic?" he asked

"Yes, but it's a secret okay? Nobody can know that you have it. Keep it in your pocket and a part of me will always be with you and you'll have some of my power and if you have my power, you'll never feel scared or alone again," she said.

"I wont?" he asked.

"No, you wont. Now go to sleep my love," she said kissing him again on his forehead and putting out the light. Blane settled into bed and fell fast asleep. Butch who was so intently listening at the door shuffled away quickly as to not let her know that he was at the door listening to the entire conversation.

She met him out on the beach for a warm embrace as they kissed one another. He looked her in the eyes, slumping down to his knees and putting his hands around her waist.

"Butch what are you doing?" she asked.

"I'm begging you to let me stay. I love you Izzy. More than I've ever loved any woman," he said.

"It's all an illusion. It's just how the island makes you feel, but it can make you evil. I wont do that to another human. I wont destroy you. I would rather know you're off living your life than trapped here with no other alternatives," she said putting her hands on each of his shoulders. He hugged her, tears rushing down his face.

"I'll always love you Izzy. Always. Do you understand me?" he said almost shouting. She fell to her knees at his desperate plea, holding him close to her and kissing him as they tumbled about in the sand in a fit of passion.

Upon the first glimmer of the morning sun, she knew what she had to do. Butch was still asleep on the beach as she rose up, calling upon the ocean to hear her.

"Ocean waves and water, hear me," she said. "Take this man back home."

The water churned with violence, sending up huge waves of water. Issiryth's hair illuminated with a golden light, cascading around her as she made her commands. The crashing sounds echoed throughout the morning sky, awakening both Butch and Blane from their slumber. She saw his tiny legs bouncing toward them, excited to face a new day.

"Blane? What are you doing here? Go back inside for a while," she commanded, but Blane didn't move.

Butch looked at Blane feeling a deep sense of sadness at the thought of what he must do. Issiryth tried to get Blane to go back up to the house, but he wouldn't oblige her request, only holding tight to her leg. There was still very little time to get Butch back to his life and she knew she wouldn't be able to conceal what was going to happen next. So, she didn't fight Blane's presence.

"Butch are you ready?" she asked. He nodded giving her one final kiss. She extended her hand out to him as he took it, heaving him up into the air and in the engulfing waves. As his body flew up, Blane's face turned to sadness as he screamed out.

"No! Butch! Mommy save him!" he screamed watching Butch bob in the water, unable to save himself. He waved at Blane who was visibly clutching the black bag his mother had given him the night before. "Get on the ship Butch! We'll sail away from her!"

As the words passed his lips, the bag illuminated with a

brilliant golden light. A rumbling could be heard from beneath the ocean water as the sails of a mighty ship billowed out from its surface. Butch's eyes grew wide with what he had witnessed. Issiryth's hair had given Blane some of her power. Angered by Issiryth's rejection, Butch felt betrayed as his heart grew black with longing for that lock of hair. Little did he know, that Issiryth was quite perceptive and acted fast when the ship appeared.

"She can't take you away!" Blane shouted.

"And you'll never be able to come to my island again!" she yelled to him from afar. He boarded the ship that was now sailing away from her. Placing her palms to the sky, she created a barrier around her island. Her eyes glazed over. Her stomach turned with the pang of loss. He was now free to sail the waters, but never to return.

"No mommy!" he yelled, slamming his tiny fists against her legs and body "No bring him back!"

She knelt down to comfort her son, hugging him. He fought her off crying massive tears of angst.

"How could you do that to him?" he screamed. "I hate you!"

Blane ran away to the house leaving Issiryth unable to console her precious son. She recognized his need for the love of other human beings, but at the same time, she knew it was dangerous. Butch would sail the waters, only surviving by sea as the captain of his own ship. He would never be able to return home or to his precious Izzy. All he had to live for now was the hope that perhaps someday he could get a lock of her hair and seek revenge. Blane grew up, soon forgetting that he had ever met Butch and never knowing how much love for him he once had. He kept the lock of hair in his pocket, always seeking comfort with it. Issiryth knew the potential for her son's heart to grow dark, which is why she forbade Butch from ever coming back.

So, as it was, Blane grew up never knowing a father and the perpetual pain of losing the ones he loved.

CHAPTER 14

HIS EVIL

When I woke up the next morning, I was back in Blane's house that over looked the beach on the mountainside. The old room was just as I had left it, with the aroma of breakfast filling up our noses. Blane was out of bed staring out the window, clutching a small black bag in his right hand. A tinge of excitement surged through me. *That must be the lock of hair.* I thought. There were forces of unforeseen magnitude at work here, but as always my optimism led me to believe I would be successful in retrieving it from him.

"What are we doing back here?" I asked him in a daze.

"This is our home Liza. I'm restoring the village now that you're back," he said.

"Well, I'm not staying Blane. I have to find Mom and wake her up," I responded.

"Yes, you damn well are staying," he barked, cutting into me with an intensified glare. "I have people looking for her. She'll be back."   "What about Stark?" I asked.

"What about Stark? He's been nothing, but a thorn in my side since the day that I met him. That son of a bitch is going to rot in jail," he said.

"No Blane. You can't do that to him. Please let him go. What do I have to do?" I pleaded.

"You know what you have to do Liza," he said.

"I can't do that," I responded.

"Then, he stays. It's that simple," he said.

"What's in that black bag?" I asked as if I didn't know.

"Nothing," he responded.

"There has to be something in it. You're holding on to it rather tightly. What is it?" I asked, reaching over to grab it out of his hand. Blane put it up in the air out of my reach quickly.

"It's nothing Liza. Just stop," he said, shoving it back down in his pocket.

"Why wont you tell me? How can we love one another if we keep secrets?" I asked.

"There are things about my childhood that you needn't concern yourself with. This being one of them. You may have whatever is mine except for this," he said.

"Then, give me Stark," I said.

"No Liza. I'm not giving you Stark and that's that," he snapped back.

I bowed my head down for a minute thinking of what I may do to avert his attention. His gaze toward me suddenly changed to suit me, displaying a soft and gentle nature, but I didn't trust it.

"Blane?" I asked.

"Yes, Liza dear. What is it?" he responded.

"Is Butch really evil?" I asked.

"Yes, quite evil. Why do you ask?" he said.

"Well, it's just that everyone here seems like they are in a trance or something, but he's different. He didn't seem like someone you brought over to the island," I said.

"He's not. Mother brought him over I assume before she enacted the curse," he responded.

"Well why is he on a pirate ship? It just doesn't seem like it fits here," I said.

"You ask a lot of questions my love. Butch has been traveling the seas since I was a boy. Mother never let him come near me. She said he was evil and I believed her. There's not much else I know about him other than that," he said.

Blane walked over to me, grabbing me by the waist and pulling me close to him.

"But that's enough about that. I finally have my Liza back. I love you baby," he said to me, pressing his lips gently against mine. His tongue darted into my mouth as we began to passionately make out. My arms found themselves wrapping around the back of his neck and pulling him into me as we kissed.

"No Blane, not now," I said flinging myself back onto the bed away from him.

"Please Liza. Now that you're pregnant with our baby, I just can't resist you. You're so sexy to me," he said lying down next to me and fondling my breasts. Pulling his hands down off me, I looked up at him, with my eyebrow raised as if to tell him I was in no mood.

"No Blane, not now. Maybe tonight," I responded.

"Awe come on baby. That's not nice," he said.

"Well, it will have to do for now," I said, getting up and walking toward the bathroom.

"Where are you going?" he asked shoving his hand back down into his pocket.

"To take a shower. I feel dirty," I responded, dropping my red dress off my body. There I stood, naked and vulnerable with a sudden rush of desire that hit me like a train, rendering me powerless to stop it. I looked over my shoulder, giving him a seductive stare as I opened the glass, shower door and turned on the hot water. Clouds of steam filled up the room, fogging over the glass as I stepped in one foot at a time. The water seared my skin as the droplets hit me all at once. It was a pleasant feeling however that can only be described as a comfortable pain. Blane's devilish grin appeared across his lips like the smile of a jackal. It was no secret that he was as sneaky and agile as one also. He took my cues to remove his own clothing, stepping in the shower from behind me and wrapping his arms around my waist.

I could feel his erection against my back as he moved his hands up and down my slippery body with a bar of soap. The suds made tiny bubbles on my skin as the water encouraged them to foam up and grow. As the bubbles became larger, his hands squished them against me, pushing them out from between his fingertips. I rolled my head back, resting it upon his strong shoulder and closed my eyes tightly. I reached my hand back to feel of his amazing member, squeezing it in my hand as it throbbed out for me. My hand traveled down, cupping his testicles and stroking upward on his shaft.

"That feels so good baby," he whispered in my ear, biting my earlobe. "I want to fuck you."

It was odd hearing him say that word "fuck." He wanted to "fuck me." I had never really heard such words from him in the past. It was generally more like "make love to me Liza" or "Ask me," but I had never heard him say that. I would be lying to say that hearing such assertion in his tone didn't make me madly and hopelessly aroused by him, but there was a small voice echoing in the back of my head, telling me that something may be off here.

Genuinely entrenched in the passion of this moment, I bent

myself over in front of him as the hot, steamy droplets crashed over me. I pulled his penis in my hand and guided it directly into my warm, wet pussy, allowing him to thrust into me with all his might. Placing my hands up on the colorful tile to steady myself, I did just as he asked. I let him fuck me and fuck me he did. With each powerful movement inside my slippery playground, I allowed him to penetrate me with a strong ferocity. I began to experience orgasm as he guided my hips back and forth over his large sex. My orgasm lingered though as it often had, giving me one after the next. As I screamed out, he grabbed the hair at the nape of my neck pulling my head back with it.

"You dirty girl. Do you like the way I fuck you?" he asked.

"Yes, I like the way you fuck me! Please don't stop!" I exclaimed.

The orgasms continued as he pumped me like a shotgun and fired his load inside of me. I could feel his sperm oozing out of my vagina like an overfilled tube of jelly as he slowly took his dick out of me. I could feel the raw soreness in my vagina. He had given it to me good and although he came quickly, it was indeed intense and satisfying. I rinsed myself off, careful not let the warm water sting the sensitive part of my skin. He let himself out of the shower without a word. My heart dropped. He left with the same eagerness that he had come in.

"Do you feel clean now?" he asked.

"Yes, thank you," I responded turning the water off.

"Good then," he said putting his clothes back on. "Leila's made you breakfast. I have to go."

His tone was ice cold. His eyes were sharp. His muscles tensed as his very posture became elevated and indifferent.

"I'm not hungry," I said.

"Fine, suit yourself," he said as he turned from me.

"Wait," I said. The chill of his indifference triggered my impulsivity. "Aren't you going to give me a kiss?"

"No," he sneered. His eyes were no longer soft and endearing. He had only mustered up enough desire to "fuck me" and leave. He shuffled out the door and didn't even look back over his shoulder.

My heart sank to the bottom of my stomach. I was losing my power over him and perhaps, even over myself. It was unlike Blane to show such little affection but perhaps he was tired of fighting me. I stepped out of the shower, feeling the softness of the throw rug beneath my feet. I blotted away the moisture with a nearby towel and slipped a silken robe over my body. I shook the water droplets from my wet hair, allowing it to fall over my shoulders. As I peered in the mirror, I could see my tired eyes staring back at me. *What are you doing Liza? Are you really doing this again?* I thought. *Be strong. Just be strong and don't let him win.* My feet marched on the cold tile, as I swung the door open and followed him down the hallway.

"Don't follow me I can tell you don't love me anymore which is fine, but that baby is mine," he said.

"I do..." I started.

"Save it. I know who you love and it isn't me. You're going to stay here until the baby is born and then I will raise it. Do you understand?" he said with sharp eyes cutting down to mine.

"Do you really think I'd abandon my baby?" I asked.

"You don't have much choice unless you decide to stay here with me," he said shoving his hand down into his pocket again. His eyes lit up with a dark magic.

I put my arms up around him, wrapping them around the back of his neck and pulling him into me. I pressed my body flush with his as I licked and bit my bottom lip.

"Blane, I love you. Why are you doing this?" I asked.

He closed his eyes trying to resist my advances, but it was clear that he was finding difficulty in doing so. His large hands cupped around the small of my back as he tugged ever so slightly to bring me in closer. His dark eyes illuminated with a seductive darkness as if he knew he was going to get the better of me. He was privy to my deception and wasn't one to be made a fool.

"If you loved me, you'd stay. Don't you see I'll give you your mother and even free Stark if you just agree to stay and raise the baby with me?" he said.

Defeated, I pulled my hands away from the back of his neck, allowing my arms to fall limp like spaghetti noodles. I didn't know what to say anymore.

"Breakfast is ready, " Leila said from kitchen.

"I'll let you think about it Liza dear," he said touching the tip of my nose with his index finger. "But I had better have an answer soon or I will put Stark to death for his crimes and you'll never see your mother again."

"No," I cried out loud. "Please. Why are you so cruel?"

"That's enough of that my dear," he said turning to the side and extending out his elbow. "Let's have breakfast now."

I took his arm, allowing myself to be escorted to the kitchen where Leila had prepared breakfast. My stomach churned with the uncertainty of my predicament.

"Good morning," she beamed as she poured us each some coffee. She then extended out her hand to me. "I'm Leila."

"Yes, I know who you are..." I started but I could see Blane was shaking his head . "I mean. It's nice to meet you Leila."

After I shook her hand, I sat down next to Blane, watching

her bouncing about, turning off kitchen appliances and cleaning up the dishes.

"Would you like your morning paper sir?" she asked Blane.

"No Leila. That will do. Please let us be alone a while," he said.

"Of course," she said doing a small curtsey and excusing herself.

"What have you done to her? Why did you change her back? She remembered her family," I scolded.

"I didn't do anything to Leila. She's happy serving me and she released her memories on her own accord. I would treat her the same either way," he said. I scowled at him as I shoveled a large bite of breakfast into my mouth. "Slow down now Liza. You don't want to vomit again."

Holding my spoon up, I shoveled a big helping of eggs into my mouth out of spite. I stared at him with the same scowling gaze, but as I did so, he grabbed my arm abruptly to stop me from serving myself any more food.

"Stop that now God damn it," he snapped at me. I quickly pulled my hand away from his and stood up.

"You're not my ruler Blane," I said firmly.

"Don't cross me Liza. I'm warning you," he barked.

"You're trying to make me die! I don't want to die. I want to live for my children. I want my mother to live and Stark too. Why are you doing this to us? Just let us go," I collapsed in the chair beginning to sob.

Blane would not be so quick to take pity on me this time. His demeanor had turned into an ice-cold state as he sat there witnessing my breakdown with no emotion. His stoic approach hurt more so than I thought it would considering how much I had fallen in love with him over the course of my previous stay. A part of me wanted to pacify Blane with my affection because I genuinely appreciated the payoff, but this wasn't about me or my quest for true love anymore. Because I was not getting the reaction I desired, my tears quieted into contemplation, never moving my eyes upward to make eye contact with him.

"Are you going to the village today?" I asked.

"Yes, of course. I have some things I need to fix. As you can see, I made a mess of some things. You are to stay here in this house today," he commanded.

"Why do you command me like a child? I'm not your child Blane. I'm supposed to the be woman you love," I said. It was apparent he was angry when I could see from the corner of my eye that he was balling up his fist.

"And I do. I always will, but you don't love me back. It's not something I can wrap my head around right now nor do I want to try. Just stay here for me. Okay?" he said in a low, monotone voice.

"Okay fine. I'll stay," I responded, knowing I was falsifying my intentions. He reached over to me, squeezing my hand ever so slightly.

"I do love you Liza. Please stay," he whispered.

I didn't respond this time, only giving him a glance to say that I understood his heartache. In that moment words were unnecessary if not only because I didn't have an answer, but because he accepted it for the time being. In that time, we just looked at one another, knowing the answer was ever lingering in limbo. His pause was acute as he kissed me on the forehead and left through the kitchen door.

"I'll see you soon Liza," he said from over his shoulder as he shut the door behind him.

Just as he did, Leila came through, making brief eye contact with me then busying herself with the kitchen dishes. I made my own decision to push the envelope with her memory.

"You really don't know who I am?" I asked.

"Of course I do. You're Liza. We just met," she shrugged going back to her cleaning.

"I mean you don't remember me? Like, at all?" I prodded. She stopped, looking at me with sharp eyes.

"No, I don't remember you," she said with a stern voice, her hands still busy with the kitchen dishes.

Was she lying? Why was she being so stern? I thought. She knew something she wasn't telling me. I was just certain of it.

"I'm going to ask you again. Do you remember me?" I asked.

"No," she said again in the same manner as before. Then, I remembered a line that Syble always used with me.

"You can't bullshit a bullshitter," I said.

"What in the hell is that supposed to mean?" she asked.

"You know damn well. Why are you pretending to not have your memories? Is it because of Blane? It seems like he went a little crazy after I left," I said.

"You know what Liza? I don't owe you anything, not even an explanation. I'm content with things as they are and I'm in no mood to have you fuck it up again. So, just stay out of my way and I'll stay out of yours," she said.

"You know Leila, we were friends before. You helped me. I just want to get my mom and Stark back home. I'm not here to cause harm to you or Blane," I responded.

"I don't have any fucks to give Liza. Just stay out of my way," she snapped again.

"Okay, okay," I said throwing my hands up in front of me to show a truce. "I'm going out to the beach today. Would that be alright?"

She continued cleaning the kitchen and putting away the breakfast dishes, ignoring what I had to say. It was clear she most certainly wanted absolutely nothing to do with me at all. I suppose I had to accept that, but losing friends is never quite a pleasant experience. In my emotional anguish, I found peace however, resolving that her plan to just stay out of each other's hair was likely the best solution. I had many other things to focus on anyhow. With a tip of my head to show a mutual understanding for our arrangement, I grabbed a large, wide-brimmed hat placing it ever so carefully on my head and shuffling out the kitchen door.

CHAPTER 15

CONTRACTS WITH THE PIRATE

The sun hung in the sky as it always had, rising to the attention of the day. The beautiful, clear blue ocean water shimmered as it brushed against the beach with soft waves. The warm sand peeked out from beneath my toes as it cradled my feet. I closed my eyes, relishing in the warmth of the sun as I sat down to enjoy the beauty of the my surroundings. The wind breezed through my long brown hair, causing it to be tossed about. I propped my hands up behind myself, basking in the morning sun. I wanted to take a moment of tranquility in the chaos of my uncertain future. I could fail miserably and end up killing us all, but I supposed it was a risk that had to be taken. The heart will tug at you when you least expect it, pulling you through the depths of hell just to retrieve that thing you love so dearly. People are irreplaceable and losing something you just can't replace is the tragedy of life. I would not allow tragedy to strike me down again, not after all the time I spent trying to hold on to things that were hardly worth my time. My mother was far more important than my quest for a prince charming.

The winds on the islands carried the soft whisper of mysticism, always encouraging me to use my intuition. I could feel the gentle nudging of a spiritual variety telling me it was all going to work itself out. I had wondered if Issiryth had wanted me to be successful the whole time. She agreed that Blane was a self-inflicted mistake that plagued her perfect planet with evil. This alone begged the question of whether or not the Goddess herself could be described as perfect. My perception of deities was their uncanny ability to see the future, to control, and create circumstances for their greater good. Perhaps creating a being in your image meant that they too would struggle with things that you yourself struggle with the most. In the intention of creating something for love and affection, it has no other option but to counterbalance itself with things like greed and selfishness. It's like making a copy of a copy. It's never quite as quality as the original. Why had she allowed her loneliness to overrule her and procreate with a human man? It was the same reason that I always failed at relationships or that Blane always tried to make his life right by doing more wrong. We just wanted love and to have that love reciprocated. In doing so, we bring balance to the situation by giving way to evil. Issiryth always seemed to right her wrongs, always trying to restore her island to peace. She could never quite let go of her beloved son. In her weakness, she failed herself.

Indulgence had led to the demise of purity. I wished with all my might that love could be less complicated; that I could find a world or a realm where it was as simple as finding someone who shared your laughter. Unfortunately, I had crossed time and space to find a man who was just as fucked up as everyone else. He made my heart beat with desire and my body rush with a passionate obsession. He made me feel just as other men had; hunting me until I gave in. I was always a trophy or a goal, but never considered a true equal. I had found a man who would give me anything, but perhaps being treated like a queen wasn't what it was cracked up to be. I realized that in friendship I was able to salvage a stronger bond without the expectation of maintaining my beauty. In Stark I had friendship, knowing that whether or not the sexual aspect was there, we could always find ourselves moving forward, caring for one another. In my estimation, this kind of love felt more inspired and genuine.

When Blane accused me of loving Stark instead of him, he wasn't all that off-base. Blane knew he had an invisible, yet very strong grasp over me. Perhaps it was in his magic or the fact that he was an incredibly handsome and passionate lover, but that was neither here nor there. The simple fact remained that I was torn between two men. As I continued to reel over my revelation on the beach, I could see a large steed bearing a beautiful woman with dark hair and a long flowing dress, coming toward me from the distance. I couldn't make out her facial features, but it seemed as if her intention was very well focused in my direction. Alarmed I stood up, squinting my eyes off into the distance, straining to get a better a look at her.

"Liza!" she yelled. "Liza, is that you?"

The horse's trot, turned into a gallop as she dug her heels into his side, encouraging him to catch up with me. Her wavy hair bounced about and reflected the sunlight with auburn highlights. For an instant, I thought it may be be mother coming toward me. The small shimmer of hope, caused me to race toward her with a hopeful excitement.

"Mom!" I yelled. "Mom, is that you?"

As I approached her, her horse slowed to a stop when she pulled the reins, and then I could see her face. The sinking expression of disappointment shone on my face like the reflection of the sun on the moon when there was a cloudless night. The brilliance of it was apparent, but it's appearance in the darkness was an indication that there was more than met the eye. She immediately let herself off the horse to console me, wrapping her slender arms around me.

"I'm sorry Liza. I'm not your mom. I'm so glad I found you. So much has happened," she said.

"Serena, why are you being so nice to me? I thought you hated me," I said.

"Not as much as I hate Blane. I'm so hideous like this," she said gesturing to show her new pair of legs.

"No, you look beautiful," I said, then paused, giving her a look of concern. "He has Stark."

"Oh my God," she gasped. "He's alive?"

"Yes, he's alive. Blane put him jail. What can we do? We have to get him back," I said.

"How did he survive? We watched him die. I put him in the sea to rest," she said.

"The sea doesn't put us to rest Serena. It releases us back to our dimension. He and I awoke from our slumber to find ourselves alive and well in hospital beds. Blane kept my mom though and I have to find her and let her know we can wake up," I responded.

"Well, what are we waiting for then? Let's go get him back," she said. Her eyes were wide with excitement.

"Of course I want to get him back Serena, but I have to tell you something that I'm a little concerned about," I said.

"Okay. What is it?" she asked.

"I made a deal with Butch Ryland," I began to explain.

"What?" she gasped. "Butch Rlyand? Why would you do such a thing?"

"He promised to take me to Blane if I got him a lock of Issiryth's hair," I said. Her eyes widened with anticipation of what I may say next. "He took us to Blane and traded us for gold, then told me I have three days to get it and if I don't, he'll take both Stark and I as his slaves forever. Then, Blane arrested Stark on the spot and said he'll put him death if I don't agree to stay here with him."

"Making a deal with Butch was really stupid. How do you plan to get a lock of Issiryth's hair to him anyhow?" she asked.

"Well, Blane keeps it in his pocket. I saw him with it. It's like it gives him power or something. I can take it from him," I said.

"What makes you think you can do that?" she laughed.

"I don't know. I have to," I replied.

"Okay," she said. "Why don't you get on the horse with me? We'll find Stark first and then you can get the lock of hair to Butch."

Seeing as how I had no other options, I took a deep breath, putting my trust again in the mermaid who undoubtedly didn't care for me too much. It seemed as though her transformation into human form had softened her to me a bit though, comforted in the familiarity of my face. We shared the commonality of caring for Stark and that seemed to be the glue that bound us time and time again. I took her dainty hand as I pulled myself up on her steed and seated myself. Wrapping my arms around her tiny waist to steady myself as we rode off down the beach, I felt a safety in her presence. The steady gallop of the horse as we passed by the fantastical scenery, was whimsical and reminiscent of a fairy tale. Her wavy hair bounced around in front of my face, caressing my cheek with small tickles.

"We're almost there," she said after a time of this.

"How are we going to get Stark?" I asked.

"You have your ways Liza. Have you forgotten how to shape shift already?" she asked.

"That makes me uncomfortable," I retorted.

"Your comfort is hardly the most important thing. Wouldn't you agree?" she smirked.

She was right. My comfort was the last thing I needed to worry over. Perhaps I would shape shift again if only to save Stark from Blane's cruel punishment. There was a bit of anxiety surrounding my departure from him and into the village against his wishes. Should I be discovered, he may put me death also. I knew I was his weakness, but that may not be enough to carry me through. As we approached the village, I hunched down behind her back, hiding behind the mess of her dark hair.

"Don't worry Liza, everything is back to normal now that he has you again," she assured me. "I'd actually prefer you stay. He went a little crazy after you left."

She slid down off of the horses back, extending me a kind hand in an offer to join her on the sandy beach. I took the welcomed invitation grasping her small hand again and pulling myself off the horse. Serena approached her loyal source of transportation, stroking his face and giving him a kiss.

"That'll do now boy. I'll meet you back here tonight okay?" she said to him. The horse blinked his eye at her and began to take off.

"Why did you do that? You're not going to tie him up or anything?" I asked

"No, he'll come back," she shrugged taking me by the hand and leading me to the cobblestone path that led us to the village.

"Wait," I said. "I don't know what the plan is."

"Try not to be seen by Blane. That's your plan," she said.

"I don't really know what I should try to turn into," I said.

"Nothing for now. Just lay low okay?" she said as we approached the village.

The streets were filled with rosy cheeked people, dancing and playing about in the streets. I could hear the trombones playing with accompanying woodwinds. The sweet melody of the piccalo danced about in my eardrum giving me many feel-good emotions. My body felt compelled to dance and move about as it resounded in my head.

"Stop that now Liza," she commanded. You have to focus. I shook my head.

"I'm sorry I know," I said still squeezing her hand. "What if he sees me?"

"Don't let him," she snapped. "Now the jail is just down the street by the courthouse. The problem is, Blane is the mayor and he works there."

"Well, why don't you go in after Stark?" I asked.

"I can't shape shift princess. I ain't a human. I'm native to Sedania," she said.

"Okay," I said taking some deep, cleansing breaths. The music was still playing, coaxing me into a dance, but Serena wouldn't allow it. She grabbed my arm to stop me.

"Don't be so weak minded Liza, really," she said.

Walking down the street hand-in-hand, the people didn't acknowledge us. They remained in their sedated state, walking about the streets in an ignorant bliss. It's as if they didn't even remember their own suffering. How sick was that? It was as we made our journey down the street, that I could feel my stomach churning, giving me a wave of nerves wrapped up in nausea. My breath became quick and heavy with hyperventilation. My arm swung around my stomach as I doubled over in pain.

"What's wrong Liza? Is this a human thing? Get yourself together," she said.

"It's just that..." I began running to a nearby trashcan, lowering my head, and blowing chunks. I reached up to wipe my lips looking back at a disgusted Serena. "I'm pregnant and nervous."

"Good Lord woman. That's disgusting, all of it," she scoffed.

"Let's go now."

I tried to reach out to take her hand, but she wasn't having it after my recent display of morning sickness. She crinkled her eyebrows, grimacing in disgust. I could see that despite her extension of kindness, she hadn't lost her inclination to be a mermaid at heart. From the distance, beneath the sounds of the trumpets, I could hear the bellowing laughter of a man. It was as if he could sense the powerlessness in others as his display was indicative of his wit and superiority. I hadn't often been sensitive to these kinds of things in the past, but the laughter in this place had the undertone of a passive distinction. His laughter did not fit into this category however as it was rather robust and dominant. I must have caught his eye when my sickness got the better of me because his familiar voice addressed me.

"Liza my love, what on earth is wrong with you?" he asked.

His long tangled mess of brown hair fell over his shoulders as he gave me his dazzling, pearly white smile. There was a sort of sexiness beneath the grit. Serena had stopped in her tracks at the sight of him, grabbing hold of my arm to stop our movement. Her large blue eyes stood wide open, admiring his stance. Butch Ryland was indeed a handsome man, but not one to be trusted apparently. As our eyes met, his pace slowed, locking into my gaze. Drawing closer with each beat of the drum, I could feel him as the music seeped through my bones. I could hear Serena's voice ringing in my head, urging me not be so weak minded, but it was an ever-ongoing struggle. The music played on, encouraging my hips to move about and throwing caution to wind.

"No Liza!" she exclaimed, but it was too late. I had already been swept up.

Butch pulled me in close with his arm around my waist, leading me into a sultry tango dance. Our eyes never left one another as he twirled and spun me about on the cobblestone road. The crowd divided to make room for us, admiring the synchronicity of our dance. He dipped me down with my head flung all the way back.

"Quite the dancer are you Liza?" he asked.

The truth was, I didn't know how to dance, but in this place, it didn't seem to matter too much.

"Have you got my lock of hair?" he asked pulling me close and sliding down my leg with his large hand as we danced.

"No," I mustered out as my breath had fallen heavy with desire.

"You only have another day and half you know?" he asked.

"Yes, I know that, but Stark is in jail and my mother is lost," I responded.

"Oh, Stark is in jail and my mother is lost," he mimicked as his arm rolled me out to the side.

"That's not nice," I scolded.

He held me close as my hips moved to the song. I could see Serena out of the corner of my eye, scoffing at us.

"You know I could get him out of jail. The jailer owes me a favor," he said.

"Oh is that so?" I asked. "How do you supposed we get past Blane?"

"You leave Blane to me, but you know I wont do something for nothing," he smiled dipping me down again.

"What do you want Butch? I have nothing else to offer you?" I said.

"I can forget the lock of hair if you'll get me Issiryth herself," he said.

"What do you mean? I don't know how to get Issiryth!" I exclaimed.

"Well, you've been a lot closer than anyone else. She loves that boy more than anything and he's nothing but a disgusting, evil slob," he said.

"Oh, is that so? And what are you Butch?" I asked.

"Now, Liza...tsk, tsk, tsk. Didn't your mother teach you that if you don't have anything nice to say, you shouldn't say anything at all?" he asked.

"It was a simple question," I said raising my eyebrows.

"You get Issiryth to me and I'll take it from there. All you have to do is make her think her precious baby needs her and she'll come running," he said.

"Well, if it's that simple, why don't you do it yourself?" I asked.

"She's on to me. That's why. She likes you I suspect or she would have obliterated you for breaking her laws," he said.

"Are you going to hurt her?" I asked.

"Hurt her? Good heavens no, of course not. I love her," he said. My eyes widened at him. *He loved her? Now, that was quite a twist.* I thought.

"You love her? Well, maybe she's just not that into you?" I suggested.

"We loved each other once, but I can't get into that now. Do you think you can do it Liza? If you do, I'll get you Stark and mommy," he said.

"Will you take us back to the ocean where we can go home?" I asked.

"Yes, of course," he said. "I'll get you guys back home, just get

Izzy to me. Can you do that?" he asked with a grin, pulling a new scroll from his pocket.

"Liza, No!" Serena shouted as I reached for the pen he was extending toward me.

"I don't have any other options Serena. Do you want Stark back or not?" I asked, turning to scratch my name. The music stopped.

" A day and half my dear or you and lover-boy are my slaves forever. Do you understand?" he asked.

"Yes," I sighed. Serena began pulling me away. She turned and spat on him.

"Your venom doesn't work here sweetheart," he said, then turned to address me. "Pleasure doing business with you Liza."

He walked away from us, looking mighty proud as he waltzed into the jailhouse. Serena pulled me away from the crowd, holding me by shoulders. Her eyes were intense and sharp.

"What in the hell did you just do?" she asked.

"I did something desperate. It wasn't the first time and it certainly wont be the last," I replied, shrugging her hands off of me as I turned away.

CHAPTER 16

A LONE LEAF

Making stupid decisions wasn't something all that foreign to me and I didn't see how this contract was any different. I knew there was a level of disappointment in my decision, but I took comfort in knowing I could get Stark back. I knew at this point, it was imperative that I was hidden away where Blane couldn't find me so my next priority was gathering Serena and hiding out in an alley way between the buildings. We waited. Was Butch really going to get him or was this just another trap?

"You're really stupid. You know that Liza?" she asked.

"Yes, I'm well aware of my grave errors, but for now, we know Stark is coming back. Isn't that great news?" I asked.

"Of course. I'm really happy about Stark," she said with a twinkle in her eye. "Although I do wish he didn't have a preoccupation with you,"

"He doesn't," I said rolling my eyes. "We're friends and that's all."

"Oh really?" she asked with the look of suspicion. "Have you ever kissed him?"

I thought for a while.

"Yes," I said. There was a hesitation in my trembling voice that I knew she could sense.

"Okay, and have you had sex with him?" she asked.

"Now, you're just getting personal," I said defensively.

"That would be yes.... Do you kiss and have relations with all your friends?" she asked.

"No, of course not...." I said.

"Then you aren't just friends. You've got benefits. It's just as well," she shrugged. "He's got benefits with me too. By my estimation, you and I are in the same boat. Now that I'm a human, we don't have to be as creative as we were before."

I threw my hands up in front of her.

"That's enough. I don't need to know any more. I don't care what you do with him. He and I aren't together," I said, knowing full well that there would always be a small hint of jealousy in seeing Stark with any other woman. I had craved to be with him in an odd way even though I knew I shouldn't care.

"Okay then. I rest my case," she said folding her arms.

From the distance I could hear some gentlemen chattering to one another as the familiar sound of bellowing laughter followed. It's as if they were old chums. From around the corner I could see Butch with his arm around Stark, presenting him to us like a show dog. He was more presentable than I imagined him, wearing the plaid shirt and jeans he had picked me up in. His green eyes shimmered in the sunlight as he opened each arm for the two of us.

"There are my favorite girls," he smiled.

We immediately jumped into his open embrace, flinging our arms around his neck. His strong arm around my waist was like an insurance of safety. Butch tilted his head toward us as if he had done us a favor.

"Just as promised, Liza my love. I'll see you day after tomorrow at noon," he said as he slapped Stark on the back. His heels clicked on the cobblestone as he walked away from us.

"He's a nice guy, but what does he mean by see you day after tomorrow?" he asked looking at me. I hung my head. I shifted on my feet allowing them to shuffle across the ground. I didn't want to tell him.

"I made a deal with him Stark. I have to get him Issiryth or you and I will be his slaves," I said.

Stark thought for moment about what I had said. His contemplation was clear as he pressed his fingers to his lips. Serena looked over at his face to see his reaction, but he seemed quite unaffected with the news.

"So," he shrugged. "That can't be that hard can it?"

"Are you crazy? Butch Ryland is pure evil. His contracts are ironclad. Who knows what he'll do to poor Izzy?" Serena said.

"What do you mean Serena? How do you know he's evil?" he asked.

"Because I know him. Izzy loved him once," she said.

Stark began to look more serious as a dark tone washed over his very demeanor. His eyes zeroed in on Serena as he begged the question.

"We need to know everything we can about this man. Who is he? What is he about? How does he think? He can take me, but I wont let him hurt Liza. We need your help Serena," he said.

She rolled her eyes as she often did when Stark spoke of me, giving me a grimacing look of disgust.

"I used to know him," she started. "Izzy banished him to the sea before she created Blane's island and he had no access to the land. I took pity on him and helped him for a while because he had no other means of survival."

"Tell us Serena. Please tell us everything," Stark said. I grabbed a hold of Stark's arm, looking at her equally as intently in anticipation of her remarks.

"Okay, but you guys have to swear not to tell anyone. Okay?" she asked.

"Okay," we said wide-eyed in unison. As we did, Serena began her tale.

Serena's Story

Sedania carried many hidden treasures on it's earthy island, but nothing compared to what it carried in the sea. It was captivating for many reasons. Not only did it have beautiful sea creatures in it's crystal clear blue environment, but valuable treasure within it's depths. My sisters and I used to go treasure hunting on the sea floor, but I was often left behind because I couldn't swim fast enough nor was I ever able to find anything. I would venture home empty handed as they poked fun at me for being too slow. One day, when I had enough of their teasing and tormenting, I decided to venture out on my own. Little did I know, that there was a tidal wave moving through the ocean that pushed me far beyond the reaches of my home. I was lost for days, left to fend for myself and worry that I would never see my family again.

They didn't even come searching for me. It was devastating. I thought nobody in the world would ever care for me again and all I wanted was a friend. One day, I was swimming closer to the ocean's surface, when from the distance, coming right toward me was a giant ship with one, single occupant; the captain. My curiosity prevented me from swimming away from him, so I went with the whim of my desire. I wished my sisters could have seen how quickly I swam on that day. Their jaws would have hit the ocean floor. As I neared him, I saw a handsome, welcoming face, extending his hand downward to me. Out of my grief, I took it only allowing myself to be lifted slightly from the water.

"I'm Butch," said the man with a perfect, white grin.

"I'm Serena," I responded.

"What are you doing out here all alone, love?" he asked.

"I got lost," I responded. I could tell he desired me, not knowing that I was mermaid.

"Come get on my ship then and I'll carry you home," he said with the look of lust ever present in his eyes.

"It's okay. I can swim. I just don't know which direction to take," I said showing him my mermaid tail.

"Well, I have something that can help," he said. My face lit up.

"You do? What is it? Can I have it?" I asked out of naivety.

"Well, I'm a business man," he said with an evil grin. "First, you have to do something for me."

"What? What do I have to do?" I asked. My eyes were wide with excitement. I knew being a mermaid meant I had a lot more advantages on the sea than he did. Surely he could not ask me to do anything that I could not equally reciprocate.

"I'll give you my compass. It will tell you exactly which direction to take and you'll get home to your family, but you have to bring me a treasure from the ocean floor," he said.

"Of course. I go treasure hunting with my sisters all the time!" I exclaimed.

"Okay, you have three days to bring me a red ruby," he said pulling out a scroll from his pocket.

"What is that?" I asked.

"It's a contract. You have to sign it and if you do, it's ironclad. Do you understand?" he asked.

I thought for a while about what he was saying, worried that I might be making a mistake, but I had been away from home for days and I knew I had to get back. Furthermore, a red ruby was the rarest of treasures found on the ocean floor and I knew surely one of my sisters would find it before I did. *Perhaps though, with determination, I would be able to oblige him.* I thought. Despite my better judgment, I swallowed hard, scratching my name on the scroll without first reading the fine print. He put the compass up in the air, teasing me with it before he lodged it into the ocean.

"Go fetch mermaid," he sneered as I scrambled to find it.

Luckily, I had spotted it where it landed and dove quickly enough to retrieve it. The compass was mine at last. I found my way home with it just as he had promised, but I was soon reeling in my brain how I would find the means to repay him. I wasn't certain if his ironclad bargaining was indeed ironclad, but a tinge of anxiety rushed over me. I knew I *had* to find that red ruby.

My family was not all too thrilled to see me back as the tormenting ensued once again, shunning me from the treasure hunting sports as always. So, I was again forced to venture out alone, but this time I was careful not to wander too far. I would search far and wide, but unfortunately, without the help of my sisters, I was unsuccessful. This went on for all of the first day and well into the second. I would wake up just before the rising sun and search well into the night. I began to feel hopelessly desperate at the end of the second day when it occurred to me that there was a Goddess named Issiryth who lived on the island. I remembered a time when she had bargained with me to drown her lover Sid, but I hadn't seen her since then. The other merpeople never found cause to interact with the creatures on the island, especially because they didn't believe in Issiryth or her powers. My journey may have been considered dangerous to some, but courageously I swam.

The closer I got, the more nervous I became. My head popped up out of the water as I looked around at my surroundings, then dove back down beneath again. I could see a small boy no more than seven years old sitting on the beach, looking out into the ocean water with a look of despair. He hadn't spotted me the first time I revealed my face from the surface of the water, but once I had done it a second time, he did. His eyes lit up as his little body jumped with delight. His black wavy hair, blew in the breeze while his arms made big motions toward me.

"I see you," I said to him as I neared the shallow part of the water. "Come closer."

He stepped out to meet me with a look of wonderment in his eyes.

"What's your name? Did Mother bring you here to play with me?" he asked.

"No, I swam here. My name is Serena. I'm a mermaid. See," I said showing him my tail and splashing into the water.

"Oh, wow. I've never met a mermaid before!" he exclaimed getting into the water with me to splash and play.

"Well, now you have!" I smiled. "What's your name?"

"I'm Blane," he said proudly, puffing up chest.

"It's nice to meet you. Say, do you know Issiryth?" I asked.

"Yes, of course I do! She's my mom! Do you want to see her?" he asked.

"Yes!" I exclaimed. With wide eyes, he grabbed my hand, pulling me to shore, but my giant tail tripped us up. I wasn't able to move past the shallow water. He grimaced as he tried to drag me with his small hands.

"It's not going to work Blane. I'm just too heavy," I sighed.

"Oh," he said looking down to the ground in quiet contemplation, then his eyes shot up with a look of delight as if he had a light bulb flash go off in his head. "I have something that might help!"

He ran over to the beach where he had a small satchel sitting. Lifting it up by it's bottom, he spilled all the contents out on the beach. It appeared he had some journals, pencils and small black bag. When he got hold of the bag he held it high into the air, commanding it to his will. It illuminated with the most beautiful white light I had ever seen.

"Get legs Serena. Get legs," he said.

As the words passed his lips, an odd feeling of tingles swept over my body. My mermaid tail transformed into a pair of human legs. They were quite ugly to me, but I figured if I wanted to see Issiryth, I would have to deal with it.

"Thanks, little guy," I said standing up. He had fashioned me some human clothes with his wish. He had covered me in a yellow dress that went down to my ankles. I extended my hand out to hold it as he walked me up to the house on the other side of the beach. I remember seeing her long blonde hair. Her upturned grin as she greeted us was welcoming. Her eyes were wide with perplexity as she examined me with her son.

"Serena, this isn't how I made you. Why are you here with my son?" she asked. I was shocked that she even remembered my name.

"I-I'm sorry your highness," I stammered. Blane shot out in front of me. He spread his arms wide and bowed out his chest.

"She's my friend mom and she's not from earth so, there's no need to send her back. Can I keep her. Please mom. Please," he pleaded. His little eyes were glazed over with a look of sadness.

His mother stood there speechless.

"Blane..." she started.

"It's okay," I said stepping out from behind him. "He just gave me legs so that I could come talk to you. I plan to return to the sea in due time."

"No!" he shouted. "No Serena! You can't!"

"This is all very bad Blane. You shouldn't be giving Mermaids legs. You have to change her back right now," she said with her hands on her hips.

"Wait, Issiryth, please. You have to help me, then I'll go back to sea," I pleaded.

Blane wrapped his arms around my waist, looking up at me with his little black eyes as if he could hold me in place himself. His tenacity was promising, but I knew I couldn't burden Issiryth with my presence. I could only hope she would hear out what I was trying to say to her.

"Blane, let her go," she commanded, but he wasn't eager to obey, holding me a bit tighter than before. Then, she looked up at me. "Serena, what have you done?"

"I made a bargain with Butch," I shrugged. Her shriek of horror echoed with thorough her disappointment.

"Serena, have you any idea how dangerous that is?" she asked.

"No, but I was hoping you could help me," I said.

"Serena, those scrolls he has are ironclad; they carry magic in them. He tricked a pelican into stealing them in return for some fish," she said.

"Well, what do I do?" I asked.

"It depends. What is he asking you for?" she asked.

"He wants a red ruby from the bottom of the ocean, but I can't find one. I was hoping you had one I could give to him," I said. She placed her palm on her forehead letting out a heavy sigh.

"No, I'm not giving him a red ruby. First of all, there aren't any red rubies in the ocean. Secondly, giving one to him would prove disastrous. You're going to have to pay the price Serena, I'm sorry," she said shaking her head.

Blane buried his little head in my belly and I began to hug him back, knowing I would soon face a terrible fate. More than anything I wanted Issiryth's protection, but it appeared that the scrolls she had enchanted with her magic could not be destroyed and there was nothing further she could offer me. Issiryth turned to Blane.

"Blane, mommy needs you to let Serena go and turn her back into a mermaid," she said.

"No," he resisted. "I won't do it."

"Blane, I will take back my lock of hair if you don't. This mermaid needs to go back and face what she's done," she said.

"Please mom. Don't take her away from me," he said. I knelt down to look at the young boy in the eyes, pulling a single seashell from my mermaid satchel and holding it up for him.

"Blane," I began. "Here, take this, put it up to your ear."

As he held it up to his ear, his eyes lit up.

"It's the ocean!" he exclaimed.

"Yes, it's the ocean. Now, every time you listen to it, you'll know I'm with you. I'm a mermaid and I belong in the ocean, not on dry land. I'll have to go face Butch alone. It's okay," I said.

"I don't want you to go to the bad pirate man," he whined.

"I know. I don't either, but sometimes we have to do things we don't want to because we make bad choices. It's the way things are. One day, you're going to grow up and have a beautiful wife and kids. You wont need a silly old mermaid anymore," I said.

"Okay," he said sniffling with a tear in his eye. "I'll never forget you."

Izzy smiled at me when she saw how sweetly I had interacted with Blane. I took his small, hand in mine and we walked down to the beach near the water. We sat down together in the shallow part where the waves could crash over us. Blane took the small black bag out of his pocket and closed his eyes. I could feel Izzy watching us from behind. It's as if a she were burning a hole through us with her eyeballs.

"Turn back into a mermaid Serena," he said looking at me. The bag illuminated with a shimmering, white light as my tail came back into form.

"Ahhh, good as new," I said before waving to Issiryth, giving Blane a small kiss, and pushing off back into the water.

I didn't look back at sweet Blane who so selflessly turned me back despite his desire to keep me forever. I try not to be emotional about these things. He was only a half-human child after all. What did I care? I swam about in the ocean aimlessly as day faded to night and night awoke to the brightness of day again. It was the third and final day and I knew that Butch would come to find me.

As sure as the ocean of Sedania is filled with many hidden treasures, Butch's ship came swiftly over the horizon and toward me with a determined purpose.

I closed my eyes and imagined the sweetness in Blane's face when he saw me and how much all he wanted in the world was a friend. I could relate to that feeling. We were two lone little leaves, blowing in the wind, only wishing we could be a part of the majesty of the tree where the other leaves kept each other company. We were two souls from different worlds who found each other for a small moment in time only to realize that neither of us could remedy the burden of it. It seemed as though life would be a travesty for both Bland and me, suffering from the same ailment, yet placed strategically in a scenario where we would grow to detest one another. Life here was ironic that way. Butch's ship loomed over me, with a dark, cold shadow that caused me to shudder in terror as his face looked down at me.

"Do you have my ruby Mermaid?" he asked with a sharp tone.

"No, Butch. What's my fate?" I asked in surrender. He shook his head only slightly to look at me with great disappointment.

"You make sure folks get through the portal right?" he asked.

"Yes," I said quietly.

"Well, I need a crew and you're going to help me get one Mermaid. You understand?" he said pulling out his scroll for me to read.

I was locked in to do his bidding over the next forty years; tirelessly kidnapping human souls that Izzy thought she was returning to their world and presenting them to him. Some of them escaped and got home, but others didn't. I was driven to do things I thought I would never do and working for Butch put an evil in my heart that I never knew was there. After the provisions of my contract had been satisfied, I returned to Issiryth and begged her mercy, dedicating my undying devotion to her and her purpose from then on. Little did I know that she would task Mermaids with the destruction of any man who dared to cross her boundary, but nothing was as horrible as what I had endured with Butch.

CHAPTER 17

HE FELL IN LOVE

Stark and I looked at one another in disbelief at the story that Serena had just told us. It was difficult to believe that Blane and Serena were ever once friends. It was apparent that I had bargained with someone who had no intention of losing. Furthermore, he knew how to play the game much better than I did. Issiryth wasn't mine to give and Butch knew that. I squeezed Stark's hand gently to experience a moment of safety. I looked to him for protection even though it was apparent he had very little to offer in that regard. He was just as lost in this world as I, but with his muscles clenched tightly he looked back at me, squeezing my hand with an equal ferocity.

"Okay guys. Say something," Serena said.

"I'm just a little shocked I guess. I thought you and Blane hated each other," I said.

"Well, that's a different story," she said. "He was a very nice little boy, but he grew up to be an evil man."

"Blane's not really evil. He's just lonely," I said.

Serena and Stark looked at one another as if what I had said were ridiculous.

"Really Liza?" Stark said, dropping my hand. "He put me in jail and the only reason I came back was to help you. Apparently that's a crime."

"He's just jealous of you. He'll come to his senses," I said.

They looked at one another again, each rolling their eyes at what I had said as if it was preposterous. I suppose it hurt to have them discount my empathy toward Blane, but it was understandable.

"Okay guys. I know what you're thinking," I said. "So, basically what you're saying is I have to accept my fate as Butch's slave?"

"Well, unless you give him Issiryth. I don't think anyone is really capable of that. Do you?" she asked.

"No, I suppose not," I responded.

Serena let out a heavy sigh, rolling her eyes again.

"As much as I'd like to stick around and help you guys figure this out, it's time for me to go. The last thing I need is for Blane to think I'm helping you two out," She said.

"But Serena, wait," I said stopping her. "How will we get back?"

"That's not really my problem. Is it?" she asked. Stark grabbed her by the arm.

"Serena, you don't owe us anything, but we need your help," he said gazing into her eyes. As he did so, you could see her heart melting right out of her chest like the wax of a candle.

"Okay," she mustered. "Just whistle three times like this."

She placed her fingers in her mouth, letting out a loud, ear piercing whistle that could be heard from the mountaintops.

"When you do that, a horse should come, but you have to do it three times. Got it?" she asked.

We nodded looking back at her. She turned on her heels.

"Serena wait," I said. She turned around, looking frustrated.

"What do you want?" she asked. I ran up to her, wrapping my arms around her neck.

"Thank you so much for everything. We couldn't have done it without you," I whispered in her ear. Her face lit up with affirmation, but she dared not let me know.

"You're welcome," she blurted out before walking away.

She walked away from us much in the same manner as she had swum away from Blane, never looking back. We were just humans after all. What did she care? Inside, I knew there was a small inkling of feelings resting beneath her skin, knowing that she made a difference in our lives. She just wasn't the kind of mermaid to show her emotion.

I turned to Stark, holding both of his hands firmly in mine. It felt good to have him close to me, but I knew we must escape without being seen by Blane. The people in the street were merrily dancing about as if they had never experienced the tribulation that Blane put them through. It was easy to make our way through the crowd unnoticed as with many of Blane's people, there was never a soul who saw beyond their own bubble of happiness. As we made our way through the crowd , we heard a booming voice, commanding us to stop. I wasn't sure where it came from or if it was addressing us personally, but because we had no other alternative, we stopped in our tracks. As soon as we had stopped though, something in Stark's eye told me that stopping wouldn't be an option. He gave my hand a tight grasp.

"Are you ready Liza?" he asked.

I looked at him with a question mark as he reared back to ready himself for our escape. He began sprinting off into the woods, dragging me behind him like the tin cans on a newly wed's car. My legs pumped as fast as they could carry me, not really knowing if the voice we heard was that of Blane or someone else. The leaves of the trees and foliage slapped us in the face as we passed them by. Tiring was not an option. Stark lifted his fingers up to his mouth, letting out three, large ear piercing whistles as we continued to breeze through the trees. I looked back over my shoulder to see that nobody at all was trailing us.

"Stark stop," I said, stopping at once to catch my breath. I was breathing quite laboriously at this point as I could go no further. "There's nobody chasing us. You're crazy."

We could hear rustling amongst the foliage, startling us both into one another's arms. He valiantly brushed me away to hide behind a large rock and quieted me by placing his hand over my mouth.

"Shhhh, don't say a word," he whispered, peaking out from behind the rock. "Oh, it's just you."

He stood me up, grasping my hands in his and pulling toward the commotion. There he was, our large black steed, prepared to carry us where we needed to go. Stark approached him from the side, letting him first sniff his hand then stroking his face downward to comfort him. The horse nuzzled into him as if they were old friends, fully relishing in his affection.

"That's a good boy," Stark said, extending out his hand to me. "Come on Liza."

"He seems to really like you," I said, approaching him.

"Yea," he shrugged before mounting the horse and lowering his hand to me. I took it as he pulled me up slowly flexing every muscle in his arm to assist me in mounting the horse. I straddled the beast, wrapping my arms around Stark's hard, upper body and holding him tightly next me. The feeling of the horses back, pressing against my labia combined with the firmness of his body, gave me an excitement all of its own. I inhaled Stark's scent and let it do its tantric dance as I gently breathed out on the back of his neck. I could feel him flexing and stiffening up to impress me with his strength as he dug his heels into the horse and let us gallop away into the woods.

"Do you think it was Blane who saw us?" I asked.

"I don't know. All I knew was that we had to get the hell out of there," he said.

"Well, where are we going?" I asked.

"Into the woods Liza. We have to find your mom and get the hell out of here," he said.

"What about Butch?" I asked.

"We don't have to worry about him if we make it through the portal before the deadline right?" he asked.

"Maybe we should just ask Issiryth for help," I suggested.

"Yea, you see how well that worked out for Serena," he said.

"What else can we do?" I asked.

"Get away from Blane and find your mom," he said.

I held onto him tighter, resting my head between the shoulder blades in his back. I felt a safety with him that can't often be explained in words. His very energy resounded with a promising cry, always letting me know that with him, I was safe. He would shelter me from the storm and we would navigate the rough waters together. The horse carried us deeper into the woods and away from the noise of the village, soon we could hear them no longer as in the depths of the forest, we found ourselves in a peaceful, secluded state. The sky drew darker. With the sun no longer, lighting the way to guide us along, Stark slowed down the horse and slid off of him.

"We'll have to camp here for the night. Are you alright with that?" he asked.

"As long as I'm with you, I feel safe," I blurted without thinking.

"Good, I'm glad you do. I'll always protect you Liza," he said, helping me off the horse. His strong hands fitted around my tiny waist, pulling me down to him, where I found myself wrapping my arms around his neck and gazing up into his dazzling green eyes. The horse found rest within the woods.

"Wait," I shouted to him. Stark grabbed me back toward him, urging me to forget the horse.

"Liza, stop. He'll come back," he said. I sighed out loud, looking back up at him in the same manner I had before. He brushed my long, brown hair from my eyes, pulling me in for the softness of his kiss. As our lips met each others, I could feel the warmth of his heat radiating from him like the sun in the desert. It was growing dark and quiet in the depth of the forest where all we had was one another. The stars in the sky were peaking out at us from the leaves of the trees. We held on, caressing each other as we both admired the night's sky.

"What are we doing?" I whispered. He pressed his finger up against my lip.

"We are just enjoying this moment. This moment is all that we have. There is no future or past, only the here and now. We've traveled across time and space once again, only to have the universe bring us back together. I wish you knew how you made me feel. No other woman has ever captivated me as you have," he said holding me with my shoulders scrunched up together.

I hesitated though, knowing that I couldn't love Stark with my whole heart. Not when I loved another man also. He could feel the coolness of my brush-off when I tensed up in his arms, not fully allowing myself to enjoy this moment he spoke of. My heart had been trampled on so many times and he was exactly the type of man who captured and tossed it away.

"Just be present with me Liza," he said locking me in his arms. "Just forget everything. We don't have to do anything you don't want to do."

It was an odd victory to find myself in a position where I was the one to call the shots in my own love life. This man was growing weak for me and I greeted him with indifference on the basis that my heart may belong to someone else. His ambition was slowly swaying me though. He was breaking down my walls bit-by-bit with the jackhammer of his love. He tempted me with his sensuality. He was firm, yet gentle in a way a man had never commanded me in the past. Moving the hair off my shoulder and back of my neck, he began to gently massage me. He drew a breath over my skin as I felt his face close to me on my neck and shoulders. His kisses pressed against me like a rose petal. It was soft to the touch and romantic in essence.

"Just be with me now," he said with a voice sounding low and sexy, teasing me into the enticing play that I knew would soon follow. My heart began to melt for him all over again, losing it's sense of conflict. Blane was slowly becoming an after-thought in this instant where I was being persuaded toward Stark.

"I don't know what to say," I said.

"Don't say anything Liza," he responded.

The way his hands wrapped around my waist said it all; that he wanted to have me. He wanted me sexually of course, but it felt like perhaps this was a bit more than just that. As the warmth of his body radiated toward me, I could feel his gentle heart. He ran his fingers through my hair, massaging my scalp and tilting my head to the side. He began to kiss my neck as the breath from his nostrils slowly teased my neck.

"I want you," he whispered in my ear. "Even if for only just now."

The tiny dots of color illuminated one-by-one as the fairies of the forest did their dance in the air of dusk. It was with the fairies that we first transformed and found ourselves knee deep in the enchantment of the island. Now, it seemed the only thing we were enchanted with, was each other. As he kissed my neck, I could feel myself giving in to his seduction. I turned around to face him, placing my arms around his neck.

"You don't do the girlfriend thing. I don't know what this is, but I'm confused," I blurted, breaking down the mood with my reality check.

"Why does it have to be anything Liza? I'm a man and you're a woman. There's a mutual attraction here. Why do you question that?" he asked.

"Because, I'm afraid when we get back, I'll love you, but I'll always wonder what could have been with Blane. That's not fair to either one of us," I said.

"I probably shouldn't be saying this, but I haven't truly felt alive with a woman in seven years since I broke up with my last girlfriend. I haven't wanted to feel or to have a relationship with anyone, but coming here and meeting you has changed literally everything. You think Blane can love you, but he can't. Even if he could, you've already decided you wont stay here with him. I can't promise you tomorrow Liza, but I can promise you that I don't want any other woman. If you gave me the chance, I'd love you with ever fiber of my being and I'd never let you go," he said.

"What about the children Stark? They're not yours," I said.

"I already told you, anyone would be crazy not to love you or your children. When I met them, I just felt like I was where I was supposed to be. I can't explain it. It just happened," he said.

"This isn't the Stark I met in the cove. What's happened to you?" I asked.

"I fell in love with a frustrating, complicated, mess of a

woman," he responded.

I chuckled at that. When he met me, I was desperate to get my children back, disregarding any of his warnings regarding the boat or the boundary. I looked down at the ground, a bit nervous, realizing I hadn't let him know that I was pregnant with another child. I wondered how he would take the news, but I supposed now was as a good a time as any to let him know.

"Stark, I have something to tell you," I said with a knot in my stomach. He held me close to him, placing my head on his chest.

"You can tell me anything," he said rubbing my back.

"I'm pregnant," I responded. He suddenly stopped rubbing me, placing me out in front of him with a wide-eyed expression.

"What? How do you know? We only had sex one time," he began to panic.

"Relax. The baby isn't yours. I was already pregnant when we...." I started.

"Wait, you knew you were pregnant when we had sex in your apartment?" he asked.

"Well, yes, but I wasn't really thinking of that. It just sort of happened so fast," I responded. Stark put his hands down and began pacing back and forth, swatting the fairies away from him like flies. He didn't appear to be taking the news all that well.

"Who's baby is it?" he asked.

"Well....I don't know for sure...." I started.

"For God's sake Liza. Do your relations 'just sort of happen' a lot?" he asked in a condescending tone.

"Are you accusing me of being a slut?" I asked offended.

"Well, when you don't know who the father is and judging

on how easily I got into your pants, it's pretty safe to assume that you've been with several men in a short time frame," he responded.

"Who are you to talk Stark? Serena made it clear to me that she has benefits with you. Who knows how many women you've boinked. What's your problem?" I retorted.

"You know I may act like a cocky Casanova, but I don't have sex as much as you think I do," he said looking down. He appeared to be slightly ashamed in his assumption of me.

"Okay, you know what? I'm really offended by your questions. I thought we were friends no matter what, but I guess I was wrong. I can't take back the things that I did," I said.

"I know, I get it. Let's just set-up camp and go to sleep alright? I don't want to talk about it anymore," he responded.

The fairies quickly worked to fulfill our wishes, creating a picturesque tent with a single, large queen sized mattress including plush pillows, wine, and rose petals. The romantic scene they were trying to create, was obviously not happening this evening, but we were grateful to them anyway.

"After you," he said motioning for me to get into the tent the first.

I awkwardly crawled over to one side of mattress sitting with my head down in my hands. Stark said nothing, simply crawling over to his side and lying down with his back turned to me. I began to sob to myself, feeling the burden of being an easy woman who didn't know who the father of her own child was. Stark was obviously disappointed in my transgressions as he made that quite clear in his expressions toward me. I slipped down on the bed, with my back turned to him. I was still crying to myself.

"Please cut that out Liza, I can't stand to listen to you cry," he snapped.

"I'm sorry," I whispered, trying to conceal the noises.

"I don't think you're a slut, okay? I just can't stand the thought of you being with another man. It just really infuriates me," he said.

"Well, it's not as if we were ever together. You knew I was with Blane," I responded.

"Yes, I knew that, but I knew nothing of any other man. How many men have you met on the island?" he asked.

"He wasn't a man I met on the island. He was my boyfriend back home. We broke up right before the car accident. Blane came in and swept me off my feet when I was in a vulnerable state," I responded.

"Oh. I'm sorry Liza. I really am. Just please don't cry anymore. We have to find your mom in the morning," he said.

"Okay, goodnight then," I said.

I felt the bottom of his foot touch mine, to let me know he still cared even if he didn't care to be close as this particular moment. I still cried inside, but I held my feelings back from him the best I could, falling asleep without the assurance of his continued affection.

CHAPTER 18
THE FERAL WOMAN

The morning sun greeted us as it often had with its bright radiance and friendly warmth. I found myself completely surrounded by the strength of Stark's arms, wrapped tightly around my body with his knees lodged into the back of mine. I could feel his manhood pressing on my bum with the hardness and girth of an adequate flashlight. It was apparent he had not been awakened in the same manner I had by the morning sun. There was a heaviness in his breath and tightness in his grasp of my body that sent the tingles of curiosity all over my extremities. He thrust his pelvis forward, rubbing his penis against me. He was making subtle noises of pleasure. It was exciting to me, but I didn't want to give in. I couldn't have him thinking that I always did this sort of thing. His grinding against me, combined with the strength of his grasp was almost more than I could bear. I held to his strong, muscular arm, sticking out my ass out to further his pleasure. He moaned, thrusting his bulge into me.

"God that feels good," he whispered in my ear in a half-awake, half-asleep sort of voice.

I held his hand in mine, encouraging him to cup my breast. I let out the heavy sight of desire. The rocking of his hips and feeling the hardness of him against me, teased me into a sexual frenzy. In my animal state, I reached behind me, giving his cock a gentle stroke. His hands began to travel up my dress. I pulled his underwear down around his ankles with my feet. I wasn't certain if he was awake or asleep, but he did seem quite into the exchange none-the-less. We were naked, spooning, and rubbing.

That was enough for me. I could hear his breath becoming rapid as it breezed across my back. My vagina was wet and dripping with the desire for his hard, steel cock. I spread my legs, guiding him into me with my hand. His hands squeezed my breasts as his slow movements began to go in and out. With each thrust, I let out a moan.

"Oh God. You're so fucking sexy," he said, kissing the back of my neck. He rocked in and out little faster this time. "You're going to make me cum."

His fingers gripped my arm. The sweeping sensation of pleasure ran across me. He held still. His hot breath blew against the bare skin of my back.

"Please don't stop," I begged.

He rolled me over on my back, exposing a full, frontal view of my naked body. His eyes sparkled with passion. His hand took my entire breast in it as he lower his head down. His tounge danced on my nipple, allowing his teeth to take a nibble. He plunged his finger inside of me, playing my clit with his thumb. He pulled my hips into him. I squirmed with delight. My hips jutted upward. Each of my cheeks rested in his strong hands as he pulled my clit up to his mouth.

"God your pussy tastes like heaven," he said. He put his finger down into my mouth. I sealed my lips over it. I could taste myself. "You like the way your pussy tastes?"

"Yea baby," I responded.

"God, I want to fuck you right now," he said.

He took his penis in his own hand, guiding it back inside of me and pushing down hard. He fucked me with the intensity of purpose. The feel of him inside of me was unlike any other man I had ever experienced. I screamed out as the first orgasm rushed through my sex and sent tingles down through my toes. Then the second came and the third.

"Yea baby, you like the way I fuck you?" he asked. Out of breath, I nodded. He slid his cock out, rolling me over on my stomach. I could feel the breeze blowing over the bare skin of my back and ass.

"Please don't stop," I begged him. His kisses teased my back and shoulders. Again he guided his dick inside of me, pushing down hard. He entered me from behind He grabbed my breasts, pulling me in for deeper, more pleasurable thrusts. I screamed out again having a fourth and fifth orgasm. The tingles shot down my legs like electricity.

"Oh yea baby. I like the way you fuck me hard!" I exclaimed. In my excitement, he pumped on me harder and faster, knowing that he wouldn't be able to last much longer.

"God you're going to make me cum," he said pulling out his cock again. I could feel the semen emptying out on my ass as he screamed out in relief, then delivering a playful smack. He rolled over next to me, quite out of breath at our recent turn of events.

"What a way to wake up," he said, putting his hand on his chest over his labored breathing.

"I'm sorry. It's just that you were rubbing on me and I couldn't help..." I started.

He brushed my hair out of my face, kissing me on my mouth to hush me.

"Never be sorry for that. I loved it," he said, pulling me in to lay on his chest. His large arms surrounded me with comfort and safety as he traced his finger up and down my spine.

"Thank you," I whispered, putting my hand back on his chest. I could feel his chest hairs beneath my hand as I gave it a tender a rub.

"I don't care about the past Liza. I really don't. I just know that I want to be with you, but it's beyond that. It's like I know that I'm supposed to be with you and I've never been more comforted in anyone else's arms. I put up a strong front, but you've penetrated my fortress," he said.

I couldn't help but melt in his words, drinking in everything he said like a chocolate milkshake after a sugar-free diet. There was something in his tone and energy that let me know he would always be there no matter what capacity or form that our relationship took in the future. I sunk into his cuddle as our naked bodies stuck together, relishing in the joy of one another. I knew it would be short-lived however because we still had quite a journey ahead of us with very little time to resolve our issues. We could hear a rustling in the bushes from outside that not only startled us in the moment, but also put us on high alert. There was no doubt that Blane would be in search of us and when he found us, there was no telling what he would do. Not only were we wanted by Blane, but Butch as well. How would we outsmart the both of them? Stark scrambled to get his clothes back on, throwing me my dress. He put his hand up behind him to protect me from whatever may be lurking outside.

"Stay here Liza. I won't let anyone hurt you," he said. I peered from behind him, pushing through the strength in his arm.

"You're not facing anything alone," I insisted, pushing through him to see outside of the tent. He turned around to look at me like a school teacher scolding an unruly student.

"Stay here Liza," he said again sternly, leaving me behind in the tent.

I didn't like being told what to do as if I were a child, but I understood why he found cause to command me in such a way. He was only trying to protect me from what may be lurking in the forest. My curiosity often didn't allow me to listen to anyone or anything and I had the same sense of needing to protect him. I tiptoed out of the tent to have a look around, but could see no sight of Stark. I held there still, swiveling my head around to take a look at my surroundings. I could hear continued rustling from far behind me.

"Come here. It's okay. I wont hurt you," I could hear him say.

The calm, caring tone of his voice, led me to believe that whatever he had found was not threatening at all. So, I found further cause to disregard his wishes and see for myself what may be lurking behind the leaves of the trees. I tiptoed, but the branches still cracked beneath my feet.

"Stay back Liza," he said, as he was huddled over something in the forest. I could hear small whimpers of pain coming what sounded like a frail woman or a child.

"What's going on?" I asked, coming to get a closer look at who or what he had. He was still huddled over the person, and I couldn't see. "Stark, let me see!"

He moved out of my way, once I pulled his shoulder back to look. There before my eyes was what appeared to be an injured feral woman. Her hair and face were covered in dirt as she sobbed holding her leg.

"We have to help her Stark," I pleaded.

"Agreed," he said looking back at me and picking her up like a baby. "I hear the sound of a stream, there must be a spring close by. Let's get her cleaned up."

As he carried her through the woods, I kept my hand on her head. She was crying and burying her head in the safety of his chest.

"It's going to be alright. We wont let anyone hurt you," I comforted.

As we walked through the forest, I could tell that it was growing difficult to keep carrying her, but Stark pressed on. We followed the sound of the spring water and sure enough, we came upon it. He placed her in the water and she began to scream out loud. Her arms and legs flailed about.

"It's okay. We're trying to help you," I said. She was fighting and screaming with all her might. My arms wrapped around her flailing body. Water splashed up in my face and soaked us both. I tilted my head toward her, humming a beautiful tune. I could feel her body relaxing in my arms as she grew mesmerized by the sound of my voice. Her screaming quieted into soft sobs. Stark began to wash her leg. He ripped a piece of his shirt off, exposing his washboard abs. Wrapping it around her leg, he stopped the bleeding. I scooped water up in my hands, allowing it trickle over her face and hair. The dirty water streamed off revealing her peach colored skin. Beneath the grime she had a smooth, creamy complexion. This wasn't a feral woman after all. It was a woman I knew quite well. A woman with all the strength in the world. When I recognized her, I stopped at once. My arms constricted around her as tears came streaming down my face.

"Mom. We found you mom. We found you. Are you okay?" I asked kissing her on her face.

Her arms hugged me back.

"My Liza. I found you. I finally found you," she said out of breath. We hugged one another for a while. Stark was a bit overcome with emotion, wiping away tears from his own eyes as he saw us embracing. I'm sure he didn't want me to see how he was feeling, but it was as sweet a victory to having found her to begin with.

"Mom, you're in a coma. You have to wake up so that you can come home. We've got to get out to the ocean as soon as possible," I said.

"No, Liza. I'm tired. I just want to sleep for a while. I can't go anywhere. I've been looking for you for days," she said.

"Mom please. We have to. They're looking for us. If they find us, they'll hurt us," I pleaded.

"No Liza," she said. Her body relaxed as her eyes began to roll upward. Her head fell backward. Her body was limp and loose. I began to give her cheek a slight slap.

"Mom wake-up! Please wake-up!" I pleaded. She would open her eyes for an instant and then allow them to roll back asleep once more.

"It's no use Liza. She can't travel like this. We'll have to take her back to camp and let her regain her strength a while. We can press on later," he said.

"But what about Blane?" I asked. "He's looking for us. He'll probably kill you when and if he finds you."

"I can handle Blane," he said. His arms embraced my mother, throwing her over his shoulder like a rag doll. Her arms hung down. Her face was pale and sickly.

"Let's go Liza," he commanded.

I nodded, placing my faith in his hands once more. He was putting himself last again. I wondered how I would have ever managed without him. As we got back to camp, my mothers body was frail and limp. His hand gave her a gentle cradle as he placed her down on the bed, pulling the covers up to her chin. I was thankful she was at least still breathing. I laid next to her, my hand stroking her hair. I pressed my lips against her forehead.

"Please come back to me mom. I can't raise the boys without you," I whispered.

"Liza," said Stark with a booming voice. "Come along now.

Let's let her rest."

He extended out his hand for me to take it, helping me out from the tent. He pulled me in close for a hug as I cried on his shoulder. He stroked my head, allowing it to rest on his strong chest. I could hear the rhythm of his heartbeat.

"It's okay baby. She's going to be okay. Don't worry. I won't let anything happen to either one of you okay?" he said.

I looked up at him as he wiped the tears from eyes.

"What if she doesn't want to wake up? I didn't think of that. I didn't even think that would be an issue. She seems like she's in bad shape," I said.

"It's going to be okay," he reiterated. "I wont let anything happen to you guys. I promise. He'll have to kill me first."

I could hear a rustling coming from the tent. My body shot around as I darted back inside.

"Mom are you okay?" I asked, but she didn't wake.

"Come on Liza. Let's go. Let's go for a walk," Stark said. "You need to get your mind off of all of this."

"And leave her here after I finally found her? No way!" I exclaimed.

"Come on baby. She's just going to sleep and you need to get your mind off things," he said.

I again obliged his wishes, with hesitation, leaving my mother's side. He took my hand, interlocking it in his, pulling me on the path in the woods. A walk was the last thing I needed.

"It's you and me against the world now," he said.

I had longed to hear those words from the lips of a man since my first marriage. It had always felt like it was me with the whole world on my shoulders. There was never that solid guy who would help me weather the storms or face the challenges of life. It was me and that condescending tone from men telling me how I had chosen women's rights and I deserved to do it on my own because I could. The thing is, I enjoyed traditional gender roles and I never wanted to be thrust into a world where I had to carry all the burden while men came in and out of my life.

"Why are you helping me after all I've put you through?" I asked.

"I don't know. I guess because I love you," he said kissing the back of my hand.

"What if we don't make it out of here?" I asked.

"We will Liza. We're just sleeping. We'll wake-up. Your mom will wake-up and we'll get back to our normal lives," he responded.

"Blane wants to keep the baby. He's acting strange toward me though. Like I'm an object or a possession. He said he's going to keep me here until I have her," I said.

"How do you know it's going to a be girl?"

"I don't know," I shrugged. "Wishful thinking I guess."

"Blane's not taking that baby. The only place that baby is going is home with her mama," he said.

We walked along the path with the bird's chirping overhead. I looked around and inhaled the clean air around us. Things were tranquil, a little too tranquil.

"Don't you think it's odd Blane hasn't come looking for us?" I asked.

"He probably is looking for us. So what?" he asked.

"I mean. He hasn't succeeded. Don't you think that's odd?" I asked again.

"Yea, maybe it's a bit strange, but I never thought the guy was too bright anyway," he shrugged.

"Stop," I said, hitting him in the arm. "He could be listening. This is his island. He should know what's going on. He should know where we are."

"I'm not afraid of him anyway," Stark retorted, throwing out his arms to each side and tossing his head back. "Come get us Blane. I've got her now. Come and get us!"

I struggled to put his arms down as he spun around, taunting him. It scared me. I felt like Blane was watching and listening, but there we were, deep in the woods all alone.

"Stop it!" I commanded. "What if he hears you?"

"What if he hears me? Who cares? I certainly don't," he said.

I knew that Stark was being a bit cocky about things, not really calculating what his next move very well should be, but I let it go for the time being. I pushed him around as we bantered and chased one another in the woods. Perhaps in our playful state, we could get our minds off of things for a while.

CHAPTER 19
HE FOUND US

It was mid-day by now and exactly 24 hours before I would have make good on my wager with Butch. Mom was still sleeping in the tent, recovering from her injuries while Stark and I were wandering aimlessly through the woods. I figured by now we would have to get mom and make our way out to the ocean, even if it meant we had to carry her ourselves. We didn't have time to waste.

"Stark, we have to get mom out to the ocean, so that we can all wake-up. We need to go like right now. You can carry her can't you?" I asked.

"Yea, I can, but she's not going to wake up unless she wants to. Have you ever thought that maybe she doesn't want to live?" he asked.

"You don't know what you're fucking talking about. Shut your mouth right now," I snapped.

"I'm not trying to upset you babe, I'm just asking if that ever occurred to you. Someone has to have the will to live, to actually live," he said.

"My mother wants to live. She wants to be with me. Why else would she have left Blane to find me?" I asked.

"I know your mom loves you, but maybe she just wanted to tell you goodbye. She seems in pretty poor shape. Who knows how she actually is back at home," he said.

"Why are you being so mean?" I asked, my eyes welling up with tears.

"I'm not being mean. I'm a very logical person. I can't help it," he said. I could feel, his large steady hand rubbing my back.

"Fuck you! Don't touch me," I shouted. I wriggled my shoulders allowing his hand to fall away.

"Baby, please. Just forget what I said. I wasn't trying to hurt your feelings," he pleaded.

"Too late," I said. The heaviness of my footsteps thudded on the ground as I marched away from him.

"Liza, wait!" he exclaimed. His strong hands wrapped around each of my shoulders, pulling me into his strong chest. "I won't ever leave you alone."

I stopped, feeling the embrace of his strong arms. My eyes were crying as the emotion was now sweeping over me. I had always succumbed to the fear of abandonment. I fell to my knees in sobs of sorrow. His body never deviated from mine, holding tight to me still and buckling to the ground with me. As we sat there in the dirt of the forest, he rocked me back and forth as he rubbed my arms. His lips gave my forehead a gentle kiss. The hum of his song sounded in my ear.

"Shhh. It's going to be okay baby. Don't worry. It's all going to be okay," he said in a gentle whisper, holding my head close to his.

We were startled by the sound of cracking twigs and fallen leaves. The footsteps of a quiet observer were lurking nearby. I could feel the clench of anxiety churning my insides like a blender. His arms constricted around me. I could feel the defense in his posture.

"Who's there?" he asked.

"It's just me. Relax," said the woman's voice.

"Show yourself," he commanded.

When from behind the trees, the familiar face of my mother appeared. She was no longer wounded or dirty. In fact she appeared to be completely restored. I felt so relieved. Her chestnut brown hair fell down over her shoulders. She wore a blue polka dotted sundress that accentuated her hourglass figure. It's as if she had never endured the hardship of the forest; she shined up like a brand new penny.

"Mom!" I exclaimed running to give her a hug. Her cherry lips turned up into a grin. Her arms were tight around me. "You're alright. You're okay. We can go back now. We can go home and wake-up."

"Just a minute now Liza. Let's think about this for a minute," she said.

"Think about what? What is there to think about? You're coming home with me," I replied.

"Will you excuse us for a minute?" she asked addressing Stark. "My daughter and I need to have a mother-daughter discussion."

"Um..." he said. His eyebrows wrinkled. He looked so confused. "Sure."

Mom's eyes followed his moving body as he walked away from us. Ensuring he was out of listening distance, she pulled me to the side. Her palms pressed me up against a nearby tree.

"Who is that man you are with Liza?" she asked

"Stark. He saved me mom. He's from back home," I replied

"I don't trust him nor do I think he's safe. We need to go alone; without him," she sneered

"Mom, no. We can't. I love him. You don't know him the way I do," I pleaded.

"I'm your mother and mother knows best. There's something off about that man and I don't think he's good for you at all. You have to listen to me. Blane can help us," she started.

"Mom are you crazy? Blane doesn't want to help us. He wants to keep me as a trophy who can bear his child. I love him in a way, but he's not from our world. He can't be there for me like I need him to. I'm not choosing death on earth for an eternity with Blane. I'm just not doing that," I said. Confusion was spinning in my mind. Could mom really think that Blane was safe?

"Listen to yourself Liza, will you? I've been here with Blane longer than you have and I know he has good intentions toward you. He loves you more than any man ever could. It doesn't make any sense why you would choose to go back to a mortal life," she said.

"Because of Jameson and Noah of course. They need me. I'm their mother," I responded, crinkling my brow.

"He could get them and we could all live here together. Why are you being so stubborn. I got caught up in his world because it's much more preferable than the hardships we face every day back on earth. It's been the best experience of my life. I don't want to go back and neither should you. Why do you want to go back to struggle to make ends meet every single day only to die a withered old woman? Why Liza? It doesn't make sense. You're fighting for something that's ridiculous," she said.

I thought for a while in a pause that must have seemed like an eternity. I couldn't really place my finger on why I was fighting to live a life that was hard instead of taking up with a man who could give me literally everything.

"Well?" she pressed.

"I don't want to live in a world that is contrived of a man's selfish desires and controlled by a lack of feeling. I may live in a world where I struggle, grow old, and die, but at least I have my own thoughts and choices. Blane wants to make us his robots here only to do his bidding and bring him all the glory and honor. I loved him despite his shortcomings, but I know I can't stay here. I refuse to raise children this way and I'd really like it if you'd come home with me," I responded.

Mom thought for a while. I hoped my words had resonated with her, but I could tell that she was going to be stubborn. She tilted her head, only giving me a puzzling gaze.

"You're such a good girl Liza. I love you so much," she said stroking my hair. "I could not have asked for better, but I think you're wrong. Things could be so different for you. I'm not leaving here though. You're going to have to take me kicking and screaming."

My heart sank to my chest at her words, which festered inside of me like souring milk. I couldn't believe what I was hearing. She wanted to stay here with Blane on his island, which meant I would have to let her die in our world. I couldn't bear the thought. It really couldn't be worse.

"Mom please," I pleaded. "Please don't do this to me. Don't do this to Noah and Jameson. You can't do this to us."

"I'm not Liza. You are. You could make this all better with a snap of your fingers, but your choosing the wrong thing," she said, grabbing my hand. "Now, how are we going to lose Stark?"

I let her hand down, looking at her in utter amazement.

"Mom, no. We aren't losing Stark. He saved me. He saved you! Who are you anyway? This isn't the mom I knew growing up!" I exclaimed.

"Oh, Liza relax. You're overreacting. I just don't think he's a good man for you to be around. He can find his way on his own," she said. Her hand began to tug at my clothes.

"Mom, no. God! This wasn't the reaction I was expecting. What's wrong with you?" I said throwing my arms down away from her. "I'm going back to Stark. I can't make you come with me, but I hope you do. I really don't want us to say goodbye this way. I came back here just to find you and you don't even seem like you appreciate it."

"I'm sorry honey," she said, stroking my arm. "Let's just think about this for a minute, okay? I don't want to hurt you."

"What is there to think about mom? I came all this way to get you, only to find that you want to stay here and you don't like Stark. You don't even have a good reason. It's that you don't like him just because," I responded. My feet marched against the ground with determination. I wasn't going to let her do this to me.

"Liza, sweetheart. Please don't be mad at me. I just want to make sure you're thinking things through," she pleaded.

"Thinking things through? I'm the only one who's been thinking about anything since we stepped through that damn portal. You've lost your mind mother and I need you to get it back!" I exclaimed.

"Let's just think about it Liza! Please!" she pleaded, still following close behind me. She gathered fistfuls of the material from my dress as she tugged on me.

I would manage to get away from her each time, swatting her off like a pesky insect. She persisted in trying to stop me however. Her behavior had me confused as it wasn't like her at all to be so adamantly against a man she barely knew. She was even supportive of my relationship with Gary. In the back of my mind I couldn't help but feel that her mind was still warped by Blane's island.

"Mom, there's something going on with you that I can't quite put my finger on, but you're not acting like yourself," I said. She scoffed placing her hand on her chest and allowing her jaw to drop.

"I'm surprised at you. This isn't the daughter I raised. I told you not to marry that boy Jace, but you did anyway. You're so disrespectful to yourself, it's disgusting," she said.

I stopped at her words, standing still in my tracks. *What had she just said to me? She never told me not to marry Jace. That was a complete and utter fabrication of the words that transpired between the two of us when I fell pregnant the first time.* My arms wrapped around my gut, wrenching in the pain of her lies.

"Mom, you never told me not to marry Jace. What are you talking about?" I asked. Her eyes narrowed toward me, glinting with an evil shine. She clenched her teeth toward me, tensing up her arms. The darkness in her demeanor terrified me. I backed away, hitting myself against a tree. She lifted up an arm at me, wrapping her fingers around my throat. Her strength was that of a gorilla. I gasped for air, choking and attempting to pry her fingers from me.

"Not so smart now. Are you Liza?" she laughed, bearing her teeth down and pressing me further into the tree. My eyes were growing dark with stars; I knew I would soon pass out from the lack of oxygen to my brain, but what concerned me further was the baby growing inside me. I managed to pull my legs out from underneath to give her a swift kick in the stomach. Her grasp was ever steadfast however, constricting me in my movement. She managed to get me to the brink of giving up, before she let up.

"Don't worry," she said. "I'm not going to kill you. I'm just reminding you who's boss."

I fell to my knees, recovering from the assault. The air could not fill my lungs fast enough. I was completely confused as to why my mother was acting this way, but I fully intended on getting to the bottom of it.

"You're not my mother are you?" I asked.

"Excuse me? Of course I am," she said.

"No you're not. You're not her. Who in the hell are you?" I asked.

"Liza, it's me. It's mom. I'm sorry I had to show who's boss, but you're being bad. It was necessary," she continued.

"Bullshit. I'm not ten-years-old. I don't need to be disciplined. Tell me who the fuck you are right now!" I exclaimed. With a second wind of strength, I pinned her against the tree. I put my arm up over her throat. She squirmed, letting out a stream of condescending laughter.

"That's cute Liza," she said, freeing herself. As she began to flee, I grasped her dress, causing her to tumble to the ground. As she did so, I saw a small black bag fall from her pocket. *It's Issiryth's hair.* I thought to myself. As she scrambled to grab it, I managed to get on top of her. We tumbled over one another, each trying to grasp it. Finally gaining the upper hand, I straddled her, holding the bag in the air like a trophy. Her smile faded into a familiar, yet different appearance. Her femininity faded away into masculinity. Her hair shortened and darkened into black. Suddenly I felt the strong grasp of his hands on my hips and the firm erection of male excitement.

"Did you really think I wouldn't find you?" he asked. Shocked I lifted myself off of him, clenching the bag firmly in my fist. Riddled with fear, I cowered, shielding my face with a trembling arm. He had aged again, but only ever so slightly. There was a hint of platinum hair plaguing his black locks.

"Blane," I whispered in a startled astonishment.

"Give it back to me Liza. That belongs to me," he said.

"And what if I don't?" I asked.

"Then I'll lose my power and I'll die," he said.

"Is that such a bad thing?" I asked. "How could you have done all this to me after you claimed to love me?"

"I do love you. I just know I can't have you and if I can't have you, then nobody will," he sneered.

"You're a dark sadistic man with a twisted sense of what love is. I will never be with you Blane. Any feelings I ever may have had are gone. You've done too much damage at this point. There's no turning back," I said.

"Give it back Liza," he said extending out his hand.

"No!" I exclaimed taking one step backward. He approached me further.

"Give it back," he said more sternly.

"No, tell me where my mother is!" I exclaimed.

"Give it back Liza and I will," he sneered.

I could hear footsteps coming up behind.

"Hey, what's going on ladies? I heard some commotion," Stark said from behind me. Once he caught sight of who was in front of me, his arm swooped around my waist, pulling me backward.

"Relax, I'm not going to hurt her. She has something that belongs to me," Blane growled.

"Well, she's not giving it back," Stark said. "Just let us go and we won't have any problems."

"I'm afraid I can't do that. I asked you nicely Liza, but you give me no other choice," he said snapping his fingers. From behind the trees there were men wearing large armored suits. They pried Stark away from me, putting cuffs on his hands. His feet drug on the ground as he tried to fight them off. They were too strong. Another approached me.

"Get back!" I yelled.

His giant armored fingers forcibly removed the black bag from my grasp. My heart sank. That was my only key to freedom.

"Tsk, Tsk," Blane said. "I thought I could trust you Liza, but I guess I can't."

"No Blane, stop. You can't do this. Let Stark go. This is my fight," I pleaded.

"Liza, it's okay. I wont let anything happen to us," Stark said. The guards drug him away with no remorse.

Blane pulled me into his arms, delivering a kiss to my cheek that repulsed and disgusted me. It was a controlling kiss, not one given out of love or affection.

"Come on now my dear. We have to get ready for an execution in the morning," he said, forcing my hands together as he bound them.

"No. Why are you doing this?" I pleaded.

"I'm not doing anything. All of this could have been avoided if you had just said yes to me in the first place. Now, I'm going to have to kill the things you love," he said.

"You're positively evil. I will never agree to stay here with you or love you ever again! Never!" I exclaimed.

"We'll see about that," he responded. He drug me through the woods as if I were a dog.

CHAPTER 20

PREPARATIONS

The tears splashed down on my pillow as I forced myself asleep to drown out the horror that was happening around me. My hands and feet were tied together, scarcely allowing me to move or get comfortable in my bed. I could see the moon shining in through a small window at the top of the stone room I was in. He had ensured I would be comfortable in a large bed, but I was very aware I was a prisoner as well. The walls were barren of any decoration and I was tightly locked in by a big steel door. I remember being drug up many flights of stairs in the black castle, but my memory was limited. I suppose I was trying to block out the trauma.

This man who Blane had become, full of evil and vengeance, is the not the man I had originally found myself loving. All the signs were firmly in place, confirming that he was indeed an abuser only after his own agenda. All the splendor and lavishing of gifts had clouded over my judgment. I knew beyond a shadow of a doubt that I had to escape, but I wasn't hopeful that I would be successful in doing so. He had me in his grasp; precisely where he wanted me. I could hear knocking at the door and rattling of keys, but I closed my eyes, pretending to sleep. Not only because I didn't want the confrontation, but because I actually wanted to be in slumber. I could hear the footsteps on the stone floor as he approached me. His hand brushed back my hair. He wiped the tears from my eyes and gave my forehead a gentle kiss.

"Poor thing. You must be tired. I love you more than anything Liza. I know you don't see that right now, but you will. Stark is just a distraction. He can't really love you or give you the things I can. I wish you could just see that I'm doing all of this for your own good and protection. My life growing up was so hard. Mother would always bring me friends, then take them away from me. I just don't want anyone else taken away. Especially not you and my child," he sobbed, seating himself next to me. He kept stroking my hair. I didn't budge.

"If you knew how badly I just want to be like everyone else in your world. I'd give up everything to be like Stark. He gets to live, have friends, have you.... I'm jealous of him. Not just because you love him, but because he's a man who can live and die in a natural way. My mother should have just given me up after she had me. She's the real villain in all of this. She's the one who indulged me, raised me, and gave me her powers. Everyone blames me, but she's the one with all the control. Nobody sees my perspective. Nobody cares about me or what I've been through. They just see the poor souls that I've hurt. The thing is, I never wanted to hurt anyone. Especially not you. I love you more than life itself and I will never forgive myself if I let you go. Never ever.... Okay, that's enough. Sleep well my sweet. All will be well tomorrow after Stark is gone. We can start our lives finally and you'll start seeing things my way. I love you," he said kissing my head again and leaving. He shut the big heavy door and locked it behind him.

I'm not sure if he knew whether or not I was sleeping, but he did speak rather freely. It was apparent that in the recesses of his obsessed mind, he actually felt as if he was doing me a favor by controlling my fate. He knew the love I had for Stark was stronger than any infatuation I may have had for him and he couldn't stand the thought of it. He felt that in his control he had power, but the truth of the matter was that in his control, he lost everything that he wanted. Love doesn't control, it allows, and if there was anything I had learned from this experience, it was just that. I closed my eyes a bit more this time, shutting myself off from the world around me. I drifted off into the blackness of sleep, never allowing a single dream to haunt nor restore me. I simply existed, suspended in time and space on a planet that had no rhyme or reason.

As the morning sun peeked through the window at the top of the stone room I found myself in quiet disrepair, contemplating how I would escape. I was startled by a thudding followed by the rattling keys and large, steel door opening. Leila was carrying a white gown over her arm and with a crown of flowers. She rolled her eyes.

"Are you up?" she sighed out loud.

"Yes, I'm up. Will you untie me? I have to use the bathroom," I said. She sighed again, approaching me and pulling out a small pocket knife. She cut the ties off my feet, but left my hands bound.

"Let's go," she said standing me up and walking me down a long, dark hall into a bathroom.

There was a large claw-foot tub in the corner and an old fashioned toilet with a pull-chain flusher. She assisted me in pulling my panties down and lifting my dress up so that I could lower myself on the toilet. I let a long, satisfying piss, moaning in the sweet relief.

"You know," I said looking at her. "You'll have to untie me if I'm going to wear that dress Blane has picked out for me."

"I know," she said looking at me with an evil glare. "Put your hands out."

I did as she said, while she cut the ties from hands.

"There now. Are you going to run away?" she asked.

"To where?" I shrugged. "I'm at your mercy."

She said nothing beginning to draw a bath and allowing the liquid soap to fall into the moving water. The bath began to form thousands of bubbles. She checked the temperature several times as it filled. I quietly observed, surrendering myself to the situation.

"Well, aren't you going to say anything?" she asked.

"What is there to say Leila? You hate me and yet here I am. You don't want me here and I don't want to be here, but Blane does. So there," I said.

"You know Liza, you should be grateful to me. Blane wanted to kill himself after you left, but I stopped him," she said.

"And why should I be grateful for that?" I asked with stoic expression.

"I thought you loved him. I saw the love in your eyes in for him," she said.

"Yes, I loved him, but he's done too much to me at this point. The damage is done. He's evil and I just want to go home," I said.

"He's not evil. He's just lonely," she said.

"Yea that's what I thought until he said he was going to kill my best friend," I said.

"He wouldn't if you'd just agree to stay here!" she exclaimed.

"I can't! Don't you know you're dead Leila? Your family will never see you again? You slit your wrists and Blane convinced you not to survive! He's fucking evil!" I lashed back at her.

She backed down for a moment, standing there still. A single tear slid down her troubled cheek. Her hand swiped it away.

"Blane is the best thing that ever happened to me," she said.

"Okay Leila. Keep telling yourself that. It's whatever. I don't care anymore. All I know is that I want to live out my life on earth as a normal person and when I die, I never want to come anywhere near this place," I said.

The bathtub was full now and she shut it off, motioning for me to get in. My eyes followed her as I removed my dress and got into the soaking bubbles. She got on her knees, grabbing the sponge to cleanse my skin, but I stopped her hand.

"I can do it myself," I said, taking it from her.

The door to the bathroom rattled open as Blane peeked his head in at me. He commanded attention, proudly arching his back and walking with a deliberate strut. Leila stood at attention, awaiting his next direction.

"Master, is there anything I can do for you?" she asked.

"Master?!" I scoffed.

"No, thank you. Could you excuse us Leila?" he asked her. She curtsied without a word obliging his request. It was in that moment I wanted to be able to pretend sleep, but it was impossible. He would always find me in a position of weakness. In his attempt at dominance he grabbed the sponge. I pulled back at it, engaging him in tug-of-war.

"Now, Liza. You can't fight me. Let it go," he barked, giving it a tug so hard that it ripped away from my grasp.

"That's a good girl," he said, beginning to scrub my skin. His words oozed like a nasty slime that wouldn't wash away with soap and water. I may have been his prisoner, but I would not submit. My slippery naked ass on the bottom of the tub, moved me slightly out of his reach.

"Why are you doing this Blane? Why?" I asked.

"Why am I doing what? You know I like to clean your naked body in the bathtub," he said moving closer to me and commencing the scrubbing again.

"If you just let us go and tell me where my mom is, we'll be on our way. You ought to be ashamed of yourself impersonating her like that," I said.

"You'll change your mind about everything soon my love," he said, moving in behind me and pulling my head back. His fingers weaved between my hair as he massaged my scalp and moved it away from my neck. He began kissing down to my shoulders, working me the way he did when he wanted to turn me on, but this time I was not eager. Instead of feeling the burn of passion, I felt the chill of disdain.

"Please stop," I said, sitting up and scooting away from him once more.

"Liza, what's the matter?" he whispered gently upon my ear with a gentle kiss.

"What do you mean what's the matter? The magic is gone now. I can't do this with you anymore," I said.

"We don't have to make love baby. Not if you don't want to," he responded grabbing my shoulders forcefully. The very manner in which he spoke rang with slight condescension. I tensed up at the physical commotion as the water splashed out the sides of the tub.

"It's not that," I said.

"Then, what could it possibly be Liza?" he asked again, squeezing my shoulders together a bit tighter. I turned to the side to look at him. His black eyes shone with no remorse. He was only filled with his own selfishness.

"It's that you're pure evil," I responded.

He threw the sponge down into the water standing up over me and placing each of his hands on the side of the tub to look me square in the eye. His eyes were still void of any remorse, lashing back at me with a vengeful sharpness.

"Yes, I am and soon you will be too," he growled. He shot up into a full stance, marching himself out of the bathroom as if the confrontation had never occurred. I could hear him down the hall instructing Leila to get me dressed and promptly ready for the execution that was to take place later. I let out a sigh of relief believing that he had gone, but the sight of Leila caused me to clench up with anxiety once more.

"Time to get out now," she said opening up a towel for me. I didn't fight her as I had been inclined to, simply because I knew that I must maintain my tranquil demeanor to make it through. She wrapped the soft, fuzzy towel around me, mopping up the moisture from my body.

"Hands up," she commanded. I did as she asked, raising my hands high in the air above her head. She jumped up, trying to get the white dress on me.

"Don't be a smart ass Liza," she said giving me a go-to-hell look as I pulled my hands down. Finally able to dress me properly, she rolled her eyes.

"I don't know why you have to dress me. I'm perfectly capable of doing it myself," I complained. She pulled my hair out from beneath the gown, allowing it flow freely over my shoulders.

"I'd much rather be doing something else. Trust me. Now let's go do your hair," she said. She sat me down in front of the vanity and began to brush my hair aggressively.

"Ow, stop that!" I said looking up at her. "That hurts!"

She just looked at me with a smirk, continuing to pull and brush the tangles in the most obnoxious manner she could. My head moved with her tugs, as I grimaced in pain. It was quite apparent, she would punish me in any manner she could. I put my hand over hers, giving her the "mom look." I had had enough of her.

"Stop!" I snapped. This time, she took me a bit more seriously. She stopped, putting the brush back down on the vanity.

"You know, it's Blane who wants you to look perfect. Not me," she said.

"I'm well aware of what Blane wants and in case you hadn't noticed, I'm not all that eager to comply," I said raising my eyebrow. She picked up the brush again, pressing it to my head and giving it a gentle stroke.

"Look, I understand where you're coming from Liza, but I'm stuck here. I have to do what he says and I have to make the most of it," she said.

"Do you ever wonder what's in the afterlife? Have you ever tried killing yourself here and seeing what happens? Forever is an awful long time," I said.

"Of course, I've thought about it, but what happened to Blane's dad seems atrocious. Who knows where he went? Can you really destroy someone's soul?" she responded.

"I don't know Leila, but it's better than being his slave. Do you see how evil and selfish he becomes? It's scary. Why do you want to live like that?" I asked.

"All I know is that my life was better after Blane took me. Whether I'm a slave or not is irrelevant. I've always had favor with him and he's never made me suffer as he has the others. I can't lose him Liza. He's all I know and I stand by him no matter what," she said.

"Has he ever tried to take you as a lover?" I asked.

"No, he made it clear that he never really saw me in that

way. It's never been a topic of discussion after that. I serve him and that's it. In return he offers me a comfortable life and protection. He gives me a life free of worry or concern. I just want to forget again. I want things to go back to what they were before, but it's been impossible since you came into my life. I resent you for that. More than you know. So, please, just do as he says. I want things to be as they were before," she pleaded.

"But Leila, I have a life back home and so does Stark. We don't deserve to be stuck here. Blane will get over me and he'll move on to greener grass," I said.

"No, not when you're the only one who can get pregnant with his child. He will never give up trying to be with you. I've never seen him love a woman more," she said.

"It's not been determined that the baby is his," I started.

"It is," she interjected. "He has the ability to sense these things. Trust me."

"Well, I don't care Leila. I'm going to go home and I'm doing it today. With my mother. Do you know where she is?" I asked. Leila looked away. I could tell she knew the answer.

"No," she whispered. I stood up, slamming the hairbrush down. My hands wrapped around both of her shoulders. She tried to look away again, but I held her close to me, gripping her as tightly as I could.

"Yes, you do! Tell me right fucking now!" I yelled.

"Liza, stop. You're hurting me!" she exclaimed. In my anger, I tightened my fist around the skin of her shoulders shaking her in front of me.

"Tell me! Tell me!" I shouted. I shook her so hard, she fell to the ground. She cowered in the corner of the room, placing her arms up over her head to protect herself.

"You had better tell me, or so help me, I'll fucking kill you!" I said. I picked up a nearby chair and rose it above my head. Her scream pierced through my eardrums. She was trembling and hiding beneath the safety of her arms. I felt the grip of strong hands clasping around the back of the chair and yanking it from my hands.

"You stop this Liza. Your fight is with me, not her," Blane's voice boomed. I could hear the clattering of the broken chair as it hit the ground with force. His big arm swooped around me, holding me back. I lunged toward her, but I could not overcome his strength.

"Go on now, Leila, get out of here he commanded," she stood up. Her mess of hair hung down around her red and crying face. Tears and snot streamed down her round cheeks. Her hand swiped it away as she got up to leave.

Blane spun me around, crashing me up against the stone wall. Each of his hands pressed my wrists on the wall overhead. His black eyes were strong as they peered into the depths of my soul with a fiery passion. His lips quivered and his eyes locked on mine with defiance. He pressed his body up against mine, struggling to keep me detained.

"What in the hell do you think you're doing? Just calm down," he said.

I moved about, finally giving into him. I held as still as possible, rolling my head to one side. Anything was better than looking at him. My breath was heavy from the physical exertion, but that didn't deter me from believing I could fight him off.

"Give me mother back Blane. Now!" I shouted. He let my arms down. His hand traced up my face and stroked the side of my head. His body was still flush with mine, forcing me up against wall.

"Now, now. That's no way to get your way with me," he said, giving my head a gentle kiss.

I was still turned away from him. The heaviness of his body against mine was arousing, but I couldn't give in to my sexual desire. There was an evil that lurked beneath the beautiful man.

"Give her back Blane. You're not going to defeat me," I whispered.

"Come again?" he growled.

"You're not going defeat me!" I shouted.

"I'm not trying to fight you, Liza. I'm trying to love you. Why can't you see that?" he asked. I sighed. How many times had I answered this question?

"If you loved me, you'd give me my mother back. Where is she?" I screamed.

"All in good time my sweet. All in good time. Now, be a good girl and put on your crown for me," he said. His body let up on me. My knees buckled, sending me tumbling to the floor. The rush of tears came streaming out of my eyes. His hands reached down, placing a flower crown on my head as I sobbed.

"Your tears aren't going to do any good Liza," he scoffed. Her turned from me. His footsteps on the stone floor resounded about the room. He shut the steel door once more. The clicking as it locked was a sad reminder of my capture. My body shot up behind him. My fists beat upon the steel door.

"Let me out! Please!! Give her back Blane! Give her back to me!" I screamed. Knowing my cries would fall on deaf ears, I fell to the ground again with my back against the door. Crying into my knees, I was just trying to think of any way out of this hopelessly, desperate situation.

CHAPTER 21

IT'S TIME

As the big salty teardrops fell on the white material of my dress, it changed from a vast white pallet, to a surface sprinkled with imperfect off-white dots. Although the surface may not have been permanently stained, it's luster had been compromised with the burden of my emotion. Much like the life I had lived, the tears may dry, but the cloth never forgets what the naked eye can't see. I had not heard a sound from behind the big steel door that imprisoned me, but I could see the sun rising in the sky, taunting me with the arrival of mid-day. Void of the stability of the world I lived in, I clung to my own knees, knowing there wasn't much else I could really hold on to other than the hope that I would find my way out.

The footsteps from down the hallway carried the rhythm of a bittersweet beat. Perhaps it was a way out or my worst nightmare. There was no way to know for sure, but without it I would remain locked away in this chamber uncertain of anything at all. The big heavy door swung open as the keys rattled to unlock it, revealing before me Blane, dressed in black from head to toe.   "Are you ready my love?" he asked extending his hand outward, to help me up. I took it, rising to my feet and wiping away my tears.

"If I must," I said, my stomach churning with the fire of lava.

He escorted me down the dark, stone stairs that led us around and around again; winding down like a spiral of infinity. As we ventured down each step, Blane's head was erect and proud. I could hear the roar of a crowd as it echoed from the large room we were approaching. It seemed as if there were thousands who had gathered there much like the same day that Stark and I had arrived with Butch. It was a somber moment. Much like the moment a death row inmate knows he's a "dead man walking."

"Come along now," he said pulling me into the room. I resisted, a bit scared of what may been awaiting us behind the big heavy double doors that separated us from it. "Let's go Liza."

The guards opened the doors for us. The roar of the crowd settled down to a gentle whisper when we came into their sight. Blane pulled me close to him. Our feet walked in rhythm with one another. The people were dressed in tattered rags again. Their faces were not just dirty, but sad and desperate. They bowed to him, but only because they were given no other choice. We walked through, approaching the platform in silence. Every eye was on us as we stood before them. Blane let my arm down. He faced the crowd, extending both arms outward.

"My loyal subjects. We have fallen once again on hard times, but Liza has returned to me," he said. They cheered at the news. He threw his hands up to silence them once again.

"She has not agreed to be my queen," he started, they silenced. Their low murmurs of disappointment, hanging on his next words. "Fear not my people, we will convince her yet. Today is a day to remind you all that if you betray me or break my laws, you will no longer have my favor. This punishable by death!"

The crowd raised their hands, cheering for him and looking to me for support. He rose his hands again to silence them.

"There are those who choose not to follow my will. My island was in perfect order. You all were happy. There was no famine or hard times, but someone put a stop to all of that. Someone betrayed me. Someone convinced my Liza not to love me anymore. Will we stand for it?" he asked.

"No!" they shouted in unison.

"What shall we do then?" he asked.

"Kill him! Kill him!" they said.

"No! Blane, Stop!" I shouted. He turned to me. His eyes were burning with anger. He pressed his finger on my lips.

"You will not address me in that manner. Not in front of my people," he snapped. He then turned to them again. "What will we do to him?"

"Kill him!" they said again, raising their hands.

"The people have spoken," he said looking to me, then snapping his fingers. At once two guards showed, dragging behind a fancy rickshaw with large golden wheels and red, velvet seats. There was room enough for the two of us and Blane again drug me behind him, urging me to sit in it. I complied with his request as I felt there was no other alternative, but hesitation wrenched inside my gut.

"Where are we going Blane?" I asked.

"You'll see," he replied waving to the cheering crowd.

The guards labored to pull the rickshaw behind them with us in it. Two large doors opened up to the long corridor leading to the outside. Villagers could be seen in all directions cheering for us as we were paraded around. There was a long, cobblestone path lined with villagers far and wide.

"Long live the king and queen," they would shout at us. I shielded my face. *I was nobody's queen. Certainly not theirs.* As we went down the cobblestone path, the bands played in a jubilant celebration. As we passed them by, I saw a tall woman with porcelain skin, not cheering at all. Her long blonde hair flowed down over her shoulders like a graceful waterfall.

"Issiryth!" I screamed, standing up. His hand wrapped around my arm, tugging me down to have a seat. I wriggled my wrist, trying to fight him off.

"Sit down Liza. Don't make a fool of me!" he snapped.

"Issiryth!" I shouted again, trying to turn around to see her. A sea of shouting villagers has swarmed around us. I could no longer see her.

"My mother isn't here and if she was, she certainly wouldn't try to help you," he snapped. "Now turn around and be a good girl."

"Why don't you just kill me too Blane? I wont let you do this," I said.

"We'll see about that," he said.

The guards were sweating and panting as they pulled us. We had finally stopped. The let us down to rest.

"Why did we stop?" I asked.

"Oh Liza, do you think we could get to the top of the volcano like that?" he asked.

"The volcano?" I asked.

"You do know that islands are made by volcanoes don't you?" he asked. His tone was condescending.

"Yes, I'm not stupid. I just don't see why we need to go on top of one," I said.

"For the execution of course," he sneered.

As he said the words, the sound of large wings could be heard flapping from overhead as a large beast landed right next to us. His talons settled into the sand as the large, fire breathing dragon bowed down to Blane in submission. I jumped back at the sight of him, startled by his large, grotesque appearance.

"Don't be scared," he assured me, stroking his big scaly neck. "He's not going to hurt you. This is Gygore."

"I don't care who he is, I'm not getting on that thing!" I exclaimed.

Blane came up to me, wrapping his hands around my waist and pulling me close to him.

"I wont let anyone or anything hurt you. Just trust me okay?" he said. He pulled my hand toward the dragon's scaly neck I allowed it, but recoiled it back almost as quickly. Blane took my hand in his, pressing it to him and forcing me to pet the dragon along with him. Gygore, closed his eyes, tilting his head back to enjoy the massage we were giving him.

"See there. Nothing is going to hurt you," he said. He nodded his head as he put his hands around my waist. He lifted me up. I swung my leg up over Gygore's large neck. Blane jumped up in front of me.

"Take flight," he commanded. The dragon's giant wings flapped in the air, as we arose from the ground. I held on tight as I scrunched my eyes closed.

The wings of the beast gave way to the wind, flapping fiercely as we took flight. I buried my head into Blane's back, fearful of what was yet to come. The trees and creatures below became tinier and more distant, making the height of the journey a bit more real and terrifying. My fingers dug into his chest, giving him the attention and ego boost that he had desired.

"Don't worry my love, he wont drop you. You'll be fine," he said.

"Why do we have to do this?" I asked.

"Just enjoy it," he yelled, throwing his head back and allowing the breeze to flow through his raven hair and tickle my face. The dragon circled through the air a few times with Blane's encouragement. The tricks may have been impressive to some, but I was not amused. My pregnancy symptoms were in full force now, not to mention the anxiety of the situation.

"That's enough now Gygore," he said pulling on his reins. "Take us to the top the volcano now buddy."

Blane stroked his big scaly neck, assuring him that he was doing right by us. My queasy stomach scarcely allowed me to do anything other than keep the scenery hidden from my eyes. I held on for dear life. Blane was enjoying all of it no less; with me seeking him for consolation and sufficiently taming a dragon to his will. He may have won in many regards, but my heart would no longer be his; not with the way he managed to fully repulse me. As we landed on top of the big volcanic mountainside the pungent smell of sulfur invaded my nose with its unforgiving aroma. I held my stomach with one hand and placed my other hand over my mouth, trying to resist the urge to vomit. Blane slid off the back of the beast, offering a hand to help me. Placing his hands around my waist, he pulled me down off the dragon, allowing my feet to lie safely on the ground. I doubled over, dry heaving in illness.

"Stop that now," he said rubbing my back. He placed a white marble in my mouth to stop the nausea. Immediately, I felt better and that alone would give him satisfaction that I didn't want him to have. None-the-less, I was grateful he had stopped me from vomiting. I stood up straight again, taking small steps backward to distance myself from the comfort of his arms.

"Thanks," I said.

"You're most welcome my precious Liza. Shall we?" he asked, reaching for my hand. I took it as he led me down a narrow path, which led us around the mountain and up to the mouth of the volcano.

"Where is he?" I asked.

"Where is who?" he responded.

"Stark. Where is he?" I asked again.

"He'll be along," he said with a menacing grin.

There were two chairs made of haunting, black twigs fashioned into what looked like two thrones. He sat me next to him, where we would witness Stark's execution. The morning sun was rising steadily in the sky, reminding me of the time line I had with Butch. I wasn't certain which was worse, my deal with him or the fact that Blane was going to have my lover killed. He squeezed my hand. Soon there was a man that came around with a large belly. He began to pound a drum that was strapped to his chest. Just as he had appeared, two large, shirtless guards also showed-up. With one in front and one behind, they carried an iron cage large enough to carry a man. In it, was my Stark. He was sitting down, hugging his knees to this chest. His head was down as desperate and hopeless as I had been. His blonde hair was matted and dirty with tattered clothes to boot. My stomach turned, distressed at his haggard appearance. My body shot up.

"Stark!" I cried out, lunging my body toward him, but Blane was quick enough to anticipate it. His arms had already given my belly a tight grasp. He pulled me toward him, covering my screaming mouth. He pressed his soft lips to my ear.

"Shhh. That's enough now. He wont be our problem anymore," he said in a low, consoling voice. Tears streamed down my cheeks as I tried to wriggle away from him unsuccessfully. Stark's head perked up, banging his fists on the cage.

"Liza! Let her go! Let her go!" he pleaded. The guard didn't take too kindly to his outburst, clocking him in the head with his elbow and knocking him out cold. Blane released my mouth, turning my body all the way around to face him and placing his arms around my waist. He dropped down to his knees, in front of me. My tears didn't cease as I continued to scream out and beg for him to stop.

"Liza, please!" he barked, pulling me close to him as he pressed his cheek on my belly. "For God's sake. Please stop this! You can stop all of this!"

Stark began to stir on the floor of the cage as if he were coming to. My head turned to look at him, but Blane turned my head back toward his again, forcing my crying eyes to try to see him through the teardrops.

"Just say you'll marry me. Say you'll stay here and be my queen and I'll spare his life," he said.

"I want my mother back Blane!" I screamed.

"I'll find her Liza. I'll give her back to you. I promise. Just please stay here with me. I'll let him go if you want me to," he said.

"You have to let my mom live too. You have to send both of them back," I said.

"Yes, Liza whatever you want. Just don't leave again. Please," he pleaded, pulling a small black box out of his pocket. His trembling hands pried it open, presenting me with an impressive diamond ring.

"No!" Stark yelled. "Don't do it Liza! Let him kill me!"

I looked over at Stark, then down at Blane. Then, back as Stark again.

"I can't let you die Stark! It's not worth it. I'll sacrifice myself so that you two can live. It's the only way," I cried, picking up the diamond and holding it out in front of me.

"No!" he yelled again, banging on the bars. The guard threatened to knock him out, rising his elbow, but Blane interjected.

"That's enough now everyone," he said raising up his hands. "What's your answer Liza? Will you? Will you marry me?"

"I, I...." I sputtered, unable to utter the words he so desperately wanted to hear. I stood there paralyzed, and unable to speak as everyone stood there in anticipation of what the next words out of my mouth would be. We were all startled in that moment as the next sound was not the words being provoked from my lips, but the song of a man.

"Yo ho, ho. It's a pirate's life for me," he sang cheerfully. "It's a pirate's life for me."

Blane stood up at once, spinning on his heels and drawing a sword from his belt, shielding me from the man who was approaching us. He put the sword out in front of him, threatening the man with death if he came any closer to us.

"Calm down Blane. Nobody is here to hurt you boy," Butch said to him. "I've come to collect on a bargain I made with the lady."

Blane put his sword back, turning around to look at me with shock, placing his hands on my shoulders and addressing me with his bulging eyes.

"Why did you make a deal with this man Liza? I told you never to do that! Why did you do that?!" he cried, then turned around to address Butch. "You can't have her. This is my island and she belongs to me! I'll give you whatever you want!"

"You know my contracts are ironclad. Quit your whining Blane. There's nothing you can do about it," he laughed, holding up the signed scroll, which illuminated in a bright orange glow.

The cage opened itself, freeing Stark at once who immediately rushed to my side. With Blane holding one arm, Stark grabbed the other as the two men engaged in a full session of tug-of war. Butch held up the scroll to us, forcing Blane to release his grip. Soon Stark and I were pulled away. We could feel the clanking of chains around our wrists and ankles.

"Guess you weren't able to get my Izzy eh?" he said to me, tickling beneath my chin. "I'll quite enjoy having you around as my slave."

"No Butch! Give her back!" Blane pleaded, paralyzed by the spell in the scroll and unable to take a single step more toward us.

His hair began to gray as he watched us leave. I could see his body growing old and hunched over as his skin dried up and wrinkled. He was nothing, but an old withered man standing there, unable to move. His gnarled hands reached out to me once more, begging for any reciprocation. I turned away from him however, repulsed by the man he had become. It wasn't because he had gotten old, but because his heart had blackened so much. I never looked back at him because I didn't want to feel an ounce of remorse. I was, in a way, thankful that Butch had given us a way out of this situation, but I still wasn't any better off I feared. We walked down the mountain, following behind Butch like robots as he sang his pirate's song, skipping along and clicking his heels together as he did so. Still clutching the diamond ring in my hand, I shoved it down into my pocket. I looked over to smiling Stark. His green eyes dazzled with a comforting expression. I had failed in my journey to find my mother, but perhaps I was never meant to come back in the first place.

"It's going to be okay now Liza. I promise," Stark whispered.

CHAPTER 22

THE SHIP SAILING IN

As Butch led us through the somber village, the people had fallen on hard times again, groveling in the streets for scraps. They moved like zombies as their faces shone with despair and disappointment. They paid us no mind as we ventured through, following behind a happy Butch who had delighted in messing with them. He pulled a mans hat off and threw it beyond his reach, making him scramble to retrieve it. It was as if the man himself couldn't really see or interact with Butch, but was very aware that his hat had been displaced. Butch did several things like this throughout our journey as a snickering Stark egged him on in approval.

"That's enough you two," I snapped.

"Awe, come on love. Live a little. If we are going to be in zombie-town, we might as well enjoy it," Butch said.

"What's going to happen to Blane?" I asked.

"Fuck Blane. Who cares?" said Stark.

"Well, his people are having a hard time, so I assume he's re-charging to keep up his appearances," Butch said in a matter-of-fact tone. "Why are you worried about him?"

"No," I said putting my head down. "I was just wondering."

"Do you still love him Liza?" Stark asked.

"No, of course not. I was just wondering," I said again.

"Well, I sure hope you don't because if you did after every-thing we've been through together, I just don't think I could ever be with you," he said.

"That's just ridiculous Stark," I said. We could see the beach in the distance as Butch's large ship was sailing in.

"Ahhh and there she is," he said extending out his hands. "My one true love."

We continued to follow along with him on the beach as the sand squished between our toes. The ship was close enough now to drop anchor as one of his crew members lowered a row boat to come out and meet us. A pirate in a red bandanna pumped his arms fiercely as he came nearer.

"Butch," I said.

"Yes love," he responded looking at me.

"Thanks," I said, reaching over to squeeze Stark's hand.

"You're welcome," he said winking back at me. It was odd because although we were now his prisoners, something felt oddly comforting about being there with him. He grabbed a key from out of his pocket.

"What are you doing?" I asked.

"Do you want to wear those chains around your wrists?" he asked us. We shook our heads no and raised up our arms to him. He inserted the key, releasing us one-by-one. Sweet relief came over me as I was freed of the chain. Stark immediately grabbed me up in his arms for a warm embrace holding me close to him, as we stood ankle deep in the water.

"I missed you so much," he said, twinkling his irresistible green eyes and brushing his soft lips against mine.

"Ah, young love. I was in love like that once," said Butch.

"Yeah? What happened?" I responded. Butch looked down into the water.

"She left me," he said in a low voice.

"I'm sorry. Is there any way you can win her back?" I asked.

"Believe me. I've tried. She doesn't want nothing to do with me," he said.

"Well, don't give up. I'm sure she's just confused," I responded.

"Ha," he laughed. "Yea you're probably right."

Stark snickered beneath his breath at my display of concern for him.

"What is it?" I asked, socking him in the stomach.

"Nothing, it's just you're really cute," he responded.

"What?" I asked again, pushing him. He teased back, giving me a tickle. We bantered in the water for a while before, I lost my balance and fell right on my butt. As he offered me his hand to help me up, I yanked him down hard as he tumbled along with me.

"This is war now!" I declared, tickling him back. We hadn't played like this in quite some time and it was refreshing to engage again in a playful way. Butch laughed a big belly laugh watching us wrestle about in the water as the waves crashed over us. Stark met me for a kiss, locking me into him. We suddenly forgot we had an audience at all as we made out.

"Liza who's that?" I heard a woman's voice say. I jumped up as if I had been caught kissing a boy I snuck in my room late at night. The voice had the familiarity of authority but the kindness of small kitten. I looked up at the red bandana pirate who had made his way over to us, but soon realized it wasn't a red bandana pirate at all. It was my mother.

"Mom!" I exclaimed running over to her and wrapping my arms around her neck. "You're here. You're okay. Mom you were with Butch the whole time?"

"Not the whole time," she said. "Who is that man you were kissing?"

"Oh," I said grabbing Stark by the arm and pulling him closer to her. "This is Stark. He saved me. We came to save you."

"Save me? What on earth for?" she asked.

"Well, because you're in a coma back at home and we wanted you to know all you have to do is wake-up. All of us were in a car accident. Do you remember mom?" I asked.

"Yes, sweetheart. I remember, but you didn't have to do all this to save me. Butch told me everything. I was just on my way back to you, but I found out you were here looking for me, so I figured I had better stay and get you away from Blane," she said.

"Butch. You saved my mom? You're a good guy? You're not evil?" I asked.

"Evil is all about your perspective I guess. I knew you guys would need my help when you said you were out looking for Blane. I couldn't very well let him keep you now could I?" he asked.

"Oh Butch!" I said running up to him and hugging his neck. "Thank you so much!"

"Okay, that's enough of that," he said patting my back and releasing me again. "We had better get in the boat and get out to the boundary before Blane sees how happy we are."

"He's right," said Stark, placing his hands in the smalls of our backs and placing us each in the boat.

Once in the boat, I found myself grasping my mom's hand with my left hand and Stark's hand with my right. I was beaming with excitement at the thought of making it back home in one piece with the ones that I loved so dearly. Stark kissed the back of my hand then, placed it back down on his lap again.

"I love you Liza," he said. "So, so, much. I'm so glad we can be together now."

My mom winked at me, squeezing my other hand as Butch rowed us to the safety of his ship. It was difficult to believe that Blane would give us up so easily without a fight, but it was apparent that even he was accountable to the laws that Issiryth had set forth. We sat in a quiet relief, the three of us as Butch continued to hum his pirate's song. I didn't understand how a man who had chosen such a lonely path could find cause to hum, but it seemed as if he made light of his situation, appreciating the man he had become. My fingers intertwined with Stark's as we drew closer to the larger ship and stopped just beneath it. Butch wedged his index fingers between each side of his mouth, letting out a loud whistle. As he did so, a pirate in his crew lowered the ropes as my mother assisted in fishing them through the pulleys. We were hoisted upward into the ship little-by-little until we were raised up enough to come to an abrupt stop. The rowboat bounced as we stopped, causing me to tumble into Stark's arms. He caught me briefly with his large hands around my waist and catching me with his sexy eyes. I had a sneaking suspicion that I would always be entranced by his seduction and he damn well knew it.

"Alright you two. I'll let you rest in the captain's quarters for a couple of hours, but after that, we'll need you to come up with a plan to get you all back to Issiryth," Butch said.

"Your quarters?" I asked.

"Yes, it's pretty apparent you two are close. I figured you want some privacy. You know our journey isn't quite over yet," he said.

"You're embarrassing me in front of my mother," I said.

"Oh Liza please. I know all about that stuff anyway. I think Butch makes a good point. You guys need to rest a while before we come up with something," she said.

"Okay," I responded, taking Butch's hand as he led me off the small boat. Stark followed close behind as if he were afraid to lose me again.

"This way," Butch said leading us to the back of the ship where there was a large wooden door that said 'Captain Ryland' on it. He opened the door to a large room with a desk on the left hand side and a giant, king-sized bed on the right. The back of the room was all window, showing us a pleasant view of the islands. The wooden floor and walls gave it a rustic charm.

"Butch, it's beautiful! How did you get all of this?" I asked.

"Oh, I have my ways," he retorted. "Have fun you two."

Butch winked at us, backing out of the room and shutting the door behind him. Stark's green eyes penetrated my soul as he looked down at me, sweeping me literally off my feet and carrying me away to the large bed. He placed me down on my back delivering small soft kisses along my neck and down to my chest. He stopped for a moment to look at me and brush my brown, silky hair from my eyes.

"You know, we don't have to make love. I would be just as happy lying here with you and resting," he said, curling up next to me and holding me near to him. He began to stroke my hair and bury his nose in my neck, but the arousal he was provoking in me wouldn't allow me to be content with only a cuddle.

"You know we don't have to just lie here and rest. I think I'm a bit too distracted with the wetness between my thighs anyway," I said rolling over and putting my hands around his neck. His face came down over mine, pressing his lips to me and kissing me with the ferocity of his passion.

"I don't want to make love to you anyway," he said, sinking his hand down in my crotch, underneath my panties.

"Oh really?" I said kissing his neck and biting his earlobe. "What is it that you want from me?"

"I want to fuck you," he said. "I want to fuck you over and over again for the rest of our lives."

Not only was I aroused at this point by his assertiveness, but the fierce commitment he had just made to me. He yanked down my panties, peeling the white dress up over my head and exposing my naked breasts. My now completely naked body was trembling with excitement as he teased me with tantric kisses around my thighs. He bit down on my clit causing me to scream out and grab fist-fulls of sheets in each hand.

"Quiet baby. They're probably listening outside the door," he said, continuing to move his tongue on my labia. I was unable to contain myself however, letting out another loud scream as he pleasured me.

"Shhhhh," he said gathering up a bit of the sheet and placing it in my mouth. He moved down to my crotch again, pleasuring me with small bites and licks. I bit down hard on the sheet as a muffled scream filled the air. I arched my back and spit the sheet out of my mouth.

"Fuck me please, just fuck me," I said, pulling on his muscular arms as he mounted me. My vagina was wet and slippery as I gave his large erect penis a gentle tug, encouraging it to penetrate me. His large cock rocked back and forth inside of me, giving my g-spot adequate stimulation. I moved my hips with him as he rammed himself inside of me. Rising up to his knees, me pulled my hips up and continued to thrust. I rested back on my neck, screaming out again and grabbing the sheets in each hand. Again, he gathered a bit of the sheet and shoved it into my mouth to quiet the noise I was making. The screams were again muffled, but not all together avoidable.

He pulled his cock out and the creamy white lubrication from my body could be seen all over him. He flipped me over on my stomach, sliding his hands between the sheets and my body, up to my breasts and grabbing them. I could feel him penetrating me from behind as he bit the back of my neck.

"Do you like that baby? Huh? Do you like it when I fuck you?" he asked.

"Don't stop. Please don't stop," I begged as he continued to pump inside of me.

"I want you on top of me Liza," he said in my ear again flipping me over and laying on his back. He pulled me on top of him, pushing my ass down as I slid up and down on his dick. The athleticism in the fucking was erotic and exciting. He slowed down after I got on top of him, kissing me and pulling my body close to him with both arms as we moved to the rhythm of each other.

"I want to make love to you now. Is that okay?" he asked his green eyes twinkling.

"Of course it is," I said looking back and giving him a passionate kiss. We held each other, kissing and moving along with one another. We tried to prolong our orgasm if only to feel the closeness of one another. The sun was setting on the horizon outside the large windows beside us as he moved in and out of me. He would start to move quickly, brimming over with the inclination of explosion only to slow his pace again.

"It's okay baby," I said. "Don't hold back."

"I just want this to last forever," he said, pushing my hair back out of my eyes.

"We can't make love forever," I giggled, moving my hips on

him. His eyes rolled to the back of his head.

"You're going to make me explode," he said, pulling me up and down on him and letting out a loud moan. I could feel his sperm oozing out of me as he came. Out of breath, I rolled off of him laying my head on the pillow.

"Thank you," I whispered, kissing his cheek adoringly.

"The pleasure was all mine sweetheart," he said rolling me over on my right side and spooning me. Exhausted from the recent turn of events and comforted by the strength of his arms, my eyes grew heavy and tired. The rising and falling of his chest as he breathed lulled me to sleep in the safety of his arms. The sun was disappearing now in the sky as we drifted away into a dream world of our own. Suddenly, I could feel his presence slipping away from me as a new presence entered the room. Issiryth was hovering over me and staring through me with her large, blue eyes.

"Why are you still here Liza? Run away," she said.

"We need you to send us back," I responded.

"Run away Liza. Don't wait for me. Just run away," she said. Her image dissipated into the air.

"No, wait! Issiryth come back! We need you!" I exclaimed, but she had vanished from me. "Stark! Where are you? Stark?!"

I could hear a thudding on the door as I awoke in a dark room. I was relieved to see Stark lying there next to me still asleep.

"Wake up babe. Someone's at the door," I said to him, shaking him awake. He sat up, rubbing his eyes and turning on the lamp beside the bed.

"We must have dozed off," he said.

"Yea, why don't you get the door?" I asked. He nodded, slipping his pants back on and opening the door just a crack as not to let whomever was on the other side see me.

"It's time to get up you two," I heard Butch say. "There's a storm headed for us and we have to prepare for it."

"What about getting to Issiryth?" Stark asked.

"We'll have to figure that out. Izzy doesn't really talk to me anymore," he said. "Can you guys get dressed and come out here?"

"Yea, just give us a minute," Stark said, closing the door behind him. "Babe, we gotta get up. There's a storm coming."

"A storm? It's Blane isn't it? He wants us to die," I responded.

"Now, that's not necessarily true," he comforted me, throwing me my dress. As I dressed myself again, the feelings of anxiety swept over me as the fear still loomed of being captured by Blane again.

CHAPTER 23

DEATH'S DOOR

The mighty pirate ship rocked back and forth as the sky filled with big heavy clouds and the darkness of night. The tossing and turning about of the ship, caused me to feel a bit queasy. I doubled over the side of the bed with a waste basket beneath me, just trying to hold it all in. As the ship would rock in one direction, I would dry heave toward the waste basket, just hoping I wouldn't embarrass myself with another display of pregnancy sickness. Stark sat next to me rubbing my back tenderly in sweet assurance. A banging came to the door that was almost as troubling as the loud thunder claps plagued us.

"Let us in mate!" Butch said from outside the door. Stark struggled with it, but managed to get it open just in time for Butch to appear with my mother in tow. We could hear the commotion of his crew outside, working to get the ship stabilized.

"I'm scared Butch. What's going to happen? Will we be able to make to Issiryth?" I asked.

"I don't know yet love, but you and Mrs. Ward ought to stay here. Stark, I need your help on deck man," he said addressing Stark. I held tightly to his arm, not ready to relinquish the safety of presence.

"Why does he have to go?" I asked.

"Liza, I'll be fine. It's just a little storm...." he began as the ship tossed us about, throwing us all to one side of the room. We lost our footing and tumbled down. The two men helped us to our feet as they made their way to the door again.

"Wait," I said grabbing Stark's arm and starring into his green eyes. "Just come back to me okay? Promise?"

"I promise," he said, giving me a small kiss. When he turned around to leave with Butch, I turned to my mother.

"Mom, do you think it's going to be okay?" I asked as I locked the big heavy door back.

"It has to be. Blane knew he couldn't keep you," she said brushing my hair out of my face and leading me over to the bed. "Lie down Liza. You look ill."

"I'm fine mom. It's just hard for me to take much more. I just want to get home," I replied with my head on the pillow. The ship tossed about as my mother tried to steady herself on the bed next to me.

"We're going to get home," she said, stroking my hair.

The rolling thunder sounded overhead as streams of lightning touched down from the sky above. I could hear the rain beating down on the ship as we we were tossed about on the bed from the movement. Mom and I held tightly to one another, trying to stay as still as we possibly could. I worried with Butch and Stark being outside trying to man the ship and wondered what horror they were facing. I wanted to just hide away from all of it, forgetting my time with Blane, but unfortunately, it just wasn't at all possible. Mom wrapped her arms tightly around me, humming softly like the whisper of butterfly wings. She gave me cause to catch my breath and calm my excited nerves.

"Shhhh. It's going to be okay," she said.

A sudden loud banging came to the locked door as if someone was trying desperately to get in. There was something invasive about it, but I trusted it must have been Butch or Stark, trying to get our attention. I stood up to open the door, but my mom pulled my arm back, causing me to stumble backward on the bed.

"Don't. They told us to stay here," she said.

"But mom, it's probably just Stark," I replied. She shook her head.

"I don't know about that," she replied. Again, the banging continued at an even more alarming volume.

"Mom, let me go," I commanded, pulling my arm free from her.

My hands pulled up the large plank that was holding the door locked as I swung it open. My eyes were ready to behold a soaking wet Stark who needed to seek comfort in my arms, but I was instead greeted with the blackness of night. When out of nowhere a tall man appeared in the doorway. He was wearing a long black trench coat with tall lace-up boots. His raven hair was slicked back and his eyes shone with laser focus in my direction. Water droplets fell from every part of him as his angry face conveyed severe frustration. Blane forced his way into the captain's cabin, forcing me up against the wall with his right arm. I could hear my mother shrieking. I could feel the coolness of his indifference as the smirk of murder passed his lips. His grip against me was paralyzing. I could see the stains of blood on his shirt collar as he let out a sinister laugh.

"Do you really think I'd let you go that easily?" he asked me.

"Let her go Blane. I don't care what you do to me, just don't hurt my mother!" I pleaded. He ignored me, relishing in my weakness. His forearm lodged in my neck, making it more constricting as I labored to keep my breath.

"Shut up Liza! That baby inside of you is mine and I'm not

letting you get way from me," he said.

"What did you do Stark? Does he know you're here?" I choked.

"I said shut up! It's my turn to talk now. Do you get me?" he said pressing his nose against mine. I held perfectly still as not to arouse any semblance of struggle. My hope was that in my submission, my loved ones would be safe. I was frightened of course, with many thoughts rushing through my head, but I complied with his request.

"Do you have any idea at all what you've put me through? Any at all? Nobody defeats me Liza. No woman has ever rejected me. I'm not letting you do that to me," he said pressing harder.

"Issiryth," I choked.

"Stop it! Shut up!" he commanded

"Issiryth," I mustered once more. "Issiryth!"

"Shut up! Don't you dare say her name!" he shouted.

"Issiryth!" I continued. Blane's face turned from cold, aggression to weak, despair. It's as if in her name there was power and suddenly his grip wasn't quite as intense as it normally was. I attempted to pry his forearm away from my neck with my feeble hands, but it proved more difficult than I had anticipated.

"Issiryth!" I said a bit louder.

"Stop it! Stop it Liza!" he yelled.

"Issiryth please!" I said in a small voice, beginning to lose the flow of oxygen to the my brain. I could see the world around beginning to go black, but I refused to pass out. I wouldn't give him that power over me. Again using my weak hands, I tried to pry his arm away from my neck, but it was again unsuccessful. As I struggled against him, I continued using her name to summon her to the ship. I knew at this point, she was the only one who could help us. As I focused on her, a bright, white light filled the room with a gentle beauty. I could see her creamy white hands appear from over his shoulder as his face melted into submission. All at once he released me, falling to his knees at the sight of his mother. I scurried away as quickly and quietly as a church mouse to accompany my mother.

"Blane what are you doing to this poor girl?" she asked.

"Mother, please forgive me," he cried, grabbing fist-fulls of her dress in his hands and using it to wipe away his own tears.

"What have you done to the men?" she asked.

"Mother please. I'm sorry. I'm sorry. Please don't punish me," he pleaded. She looked down at her son with the sad gleam of disappointment, pulling up his chin to have him look at her.

"Rise to your feet son," she said. "You're better than this."

Blane arose to his feet. Although he towered over his mother, it was clear he felt ten times smaller than she.

"What have you done? Why is she calling out to me?" she asked.

"I killed them mother. I'm sorry. I killed them," he cried. Issiryth didn't look shocked or upset with this news as she calmly addressed him again. I, however, felt a great deal of grief at this as I buried my head in my mother's shoulder and began to cry. She comforted me the best she knew how, holding me close to her, but it was a sadness all too large to resolve.

"Oh? And how did you do that?" she asked.

"With a knife. I stabbed them. They're dead," he said.

"And what do you plan to do to Liza?" she asked.

"I'm taking her back to my island to have my baby," he said.

"Is that so?" she asked rising her eyebrow.

"Yes, that's so," he replied.

"You're feeling awful brave today aren't you?" she asked.

"Yes mother," he replied, looking down at the floor in shame.

"Do you remember what happened last time you felt brave?" she asked.

"Yes," he whispered quietly. Issiryth looked over at me compassionately.

"And what is it that you want my dear?" she asked.

"I just want to go home to be with my family," I cried. She nodded turning to Blane again.

"You know Blane, when I first had the pleasure of knowing this young lady, it was apparent her love life was in disarray and the only thing she wanted in the world was to be loved by a man. You gave that to her and she really loved you back, but sometimes you have to let the things you love go. She doesn't want to be here with you. Do you understand?" she asked. Blane nodded.

"I brought a man here whom I loved very much after your father died. I loved him, you loved him, we all loved him, but I had to let him go because it was the right thing to do. When you love someone you let them go. You don't force them to stay," she said. He nodded again.

"That man whom I loved after your father. Do you remember him?" she asked. He shook his head still looking down at the wooden floor. "You saved him Blane because you didn't want him to leave, but your forcing him to stay made his life here hard. He turned evil and he did evil things to survive. You never learn your lesson Blane and you think the only way to break your curse is to make Liza love you, but you've missed the point. The problem isn't that people don't love you. The problem is that you don't love them because if you did, you'd have enough sense to let them go. You wouldn't keep them here for your own selfishness. You killed thoughtlessly and recklessly. You ought to be ashamed of yourself," she said. Blane was still stone cold looking down at the ground. Issiryth still was looking at him as if he should have some sort of explanation for what he did. His tears were streaming down as they hit the floor.

"Butch," he said.

"What about Butch?" she asked.

"He's the man you loved isn't he?" he asked.

"You do remember!" she responded. "You killed him; the man you loved more than anything in the world. You forgot him, killed him, and tossed him away like yesterday's trash. Now, I'll never have the comfort of knowing that he is safe, which is the only thing I ever wanted for him in the first place."

"I'm sorry mother. Please forgive me," he said in a low voice.

"This is beyond forgiveness son. Look at the lives you've ruined with your perfect plan of an immortal Utopian society. At least this girl was smart enough to see past your facade. Go to your island and never ever come to me again. You are not my son. You are a monster," she said looking away from him and approaching me, when from out of the darkness, came an attack on Blane quite gruesome.

A bloody Stark came up behind him placing a knife to his neck and holding him tight. Blane didn't resist or move away from him as if he fully accepted his fate.

"Say you prayers," growled Stark, as he clenched him in his arms.

"Kill me," Blane said with small breathy whisper.

"Come again?" Stark replied.

"Kill me!" he exclaimed. "Do it! Kill me! I have nothing to live for!"

His jet black hair became gray as his skin became dry and wrinkled.

"Kill me! What are you waiting for?!" he exclaimed. Issiryth put her arms out as if to guard mother and I at the sight of it, but never once pleaded for her son's life. Stark trembled as he tormented with the thought of taking another man's life despite the fact that the very man he aimed to kill had just attempted to kill him.

"No," Stark said releasing him. "I won't kill you. Just let us go and we'll never come back."

Blane thought for a moment as he looked up in his mother's concerned eyes. Perhaps, he was processing the things that she had said to him about love and he was coming to terms with the fact that he had to let us go. None-the-less, something changed in him at that moment as he gazed over at his long-lost mother for approval. Issiryth nodded her head at him in encouragement. His expression faded away into the hardship of defeat.

"Go on now Blane. Go home. I'll clean up the mess you made," she said. Blane stood still for a moment looking straight at me as I held my mother close; observing my trembling body. He glared over at Stark, then met eyes with his mother once again. Like a two-year-old who just got time-out, he collected his toys and left the sandbox in a huff. His large black boots thudded as he turned to stomp away from those of us who were still frozen in this moment of terror. I let out a sigh of relief at his departure. His absence was no longer just a distant dream, but finally a reality. Issiryth rushed over to Stark who was bleeding from his side, placing her hand over his wound.

"What are you doing?" he asked.

"Shhhhhhh," she responded, as the wound closed up and the

bleeding ceased. "There now, all better."

"That's amazing!" he said as his eyes lit up. He grabbed her hand, urging her to follow behind him. "Come on, I need your help."

Mother and I couldn't help but to follow them into the cold, dark rain as they stood over a lifeless Butch Ryland who had been wounded on his very own deck. His crew was surrounding him with somber eyes as Issiryth made her way over to him. She knelt down over him as her wet mop of blonde hair fell down around his face. Her creamy white skin was soaked by the rain and her own salty tears, which made their debut at the sight of her injured loved.

"Butch," she cried as she moved her face closer to his. "Oh Butch. I'm sorry. I'm sorry things had to be this way. I didn't mean it. If you live, you can stay. You can stay with me always."

She placed her hand on his face and moved in to give him a kiss before laying her head upon his chest, but it didn't rise and fall as a chest ought to. It simply existed there as a mass between her face and the wooden deck. She slid her hand up over his heart and arms, trying desperately to impose the same healing effect she had with my Stark.

"Can you save him?" I asked.

"Once a soul dies here in Sedania, I don't have have much control over where it goes," she said. "I'm not the only deity who wants them. You know?"

"But you have to save him Issiryth! You have to!" I screamed. "He's a good man. He saved all of us."

"I know," she said softly. The tears persisted in their pursuit of pressing beyond the eyes and descending down her porcelain cheeks. "I don't hear his heart beating."

I clenched my heart as my head hung silently. Stark and

mother did their best to wrap their arms around me in comfort and protection. The only thing I could think of in that moment is how this man would have never lost his life if I had never been there to begin with. Issiryth was always able to save my loves, but I couldn't return her the favor. As Butch lay dead there on the deck, I couldn't help but to let out a fit of tears. This was not only out of sadness, but my own remorse. I should never have let Blane love me in the first place.

"This is all my fault," I said.

"No sweetheart, if it's anyone's fault, it's mine. I should have never brought Butch here in the first place. It was selfish of me to love him, to let Blane love him, and then toss him away again. This world I created is just a bunch of selfish mistakes that were birthed in good intentions. This is my punishment and I humbly accept," she said, kissing Butch once more and placing his hands together across his chest. "Now, let's get you guys home."

Issiryth stood up, raising her hands up in the falling rain and extending them out to each side. As she did so, the rain ceased and the clouds opened up to the sky of a thousands sparkling stars, that shone down on us like twinkling lights of wonderment. The waters calmed at her command as she addressed us, offering us her hands.

"Come along now," she said as the crew separated to allow us to move forward. I had mom on one arm and Stark on the other as we approached her until we were facing her directly. She moved her hand down on my belly.

"She will be very happy with you two. She will have many blessings. Don't ever come back here. Don't ever let her know who her real father is. Okay?" she said looking up at Stark.

"What do you mean? I'm her father. That baby is mine," he replied. Issiryth smiled.

"Good then, we understand each other," she said. "Everyone

hold hands now."

We all held hands together with Issiryth as if we were about to play a game of ring around the rosies. The white light radiated from her as we did so, beginning to fade away in the surroundings. I can't quite be sure, but as the light surrounded us, dissolving anything that may have been there, I could see Butch stirring about on the deck as if he might wake up. I gasped aloud pointing, but was unable to speak in the brilliance of her light. Issiryth didn't react to my expression, but only winked as she too faded away from me. Soon the light whittled away into darkness as we journeyed back and I knew at once, I was where I belonged.

CHAPTER 24

AWAKE

In his arms again I could feel the warmth of his breath on the back of my shoulder. With each exhale, he moved me. His arm wrapped tightly around my waist as he held me close to him in a spoon. The room was still dark, but in his arms I felt his safety. A red light was beaming out at me from in front of my closed eyelids. I labored to open my eyes as I pressed my hand over his as a sweet reassurance that he hadn't left my side. The alarm clock on my bedside table illuminated with large red numbers; it was 6 am. I rolled over to look at my Stark who was still sleeping soundly next to me on my bed in the apartment.

"Stark," I whispered, trying to shake him awake. "Baby, wake up baby. We're back."

I could see him smiling as if he were only pretending to sleep in the first place. He rolled over away from me, resisting being roused from his sleep.

"Come on baby. Ten more minutes," he teased, grabbing me close to him for a snuggle.

"Stark, we have to get up. We're back. I can't believe it. We're back," I said.

My cell phone could be heard from the other room. I sprang from the bed and bounded across my bedroom floor and into the living room. My phone was vibrating on the coffee table. I scooped it up in my hands at once and swiped the answer button.

"Hello?" I said.

"Yes, may I please speak with Liza Ward?" said a lady's voice on the other end.

"Yes, this is Liza Ward. Who are you?" I asked.

"This is Nurse Linda from the hospital. There's something going on with your mother and we need you to come down to the hospital immediately," she said. My heart sank. What if it wasn't good news?

"Is something the matter? Is she okay?" I asked.

"We aren't sure yet. Can you please make your way down here?" she asked.

"Of course," I said, hanging up the phone and dropping it down on the coffee table once more. I sunk into the couch unsure of my feelings. When I had left Sedania, she seemed fine. She was ready to come home to me. What had happened? What was wrong? It was difficult to determine in the nurse's voice what, if anything at all was going on with my mother. Stark appeared in the doorway of my room rubbing his sleepy eyes as he peered out at me.

"What's going on babe?" he asked.

"It's mom. They said I need to go to the hospital immediately," I said trying not to cry.

"That's good news right?" he asked.

"I don't know. She wouldn't say," I replied.

"Well, come on then. Let's go. We don't have any time to lose," he said gathering up the keys and putting his shoes on.

The morning sun was peeking over the horizon as we clamored into Stark's car and made our way to the hospital. We didn't say much to one another as I observed the outdoor scenery going by us from out the passenger window. He placed his hand upon my knee to comfort me, but I scarcely noticed as my mind had presently occupied itself with thoughts of my mom's fate. Perhaps this was her time to die and I was simply holding on to something that I had no business trying to keep. If it's her time, then it's her time. I couldn't be so selfish to try to hold on to her and yet, I fought with everything inside of me just to save her.

"Do you think it's over now?" I asked.

"Do I think what's over now?" he responded.

"With Blane. Do you think he'll leave us alone now?" I asked.

"Yea, of course. I think he knows you love me and not him," he said kissing the back of my hand.

Did I really not love Blane anymore? Was he really gone from my heart? I suppose a very small part of myself still remembered the love we shared with one another and I felt sorry for him. I was content to spend the rest of my life with Stark and never lay eyes on Blane again, but I would never forget him. He would always occupy a place within the deep recesses of my heart; squished down so the rest of the world couldn't see it. At any moment however, he could awaken that piece of me again. It was something I would have to be careful never to utter to another soul as long as I lived. Stark was never afflicted with the worry that I may stray from him. He was like naive puppy; so trusting and bursting with unconditional love. To him I could do no wrong and in that realization, I smiled sweetly back at him.

"Of course he does," I said and turned back to look out the window once more.

As we pulled into the hospital parking lot, he released my hand as he put the car into park. He got out and walked over to my door and held it open. I took his hand and arose to stand by his side as we walked into the hospital building. I tapped my feet as the elevator made its way down and finally the doors opened. I clicked the third floor button and crossed my arms. I could feel the nervous anxiety welling up inside of me.

"It's going to be okay baby," he said, but I didn't believe him nor did I give him the satisfaction of a response. I simply stayed quiet, watching the numbers of the elevator go up one-by-one. He may have been frustrated with my blatant disregard of him, but he said nothing, allowing me to continue on my way out of the elevator without so much as a word. I could hear heels clicking on the floor as we made our way to the nurses station and turned to find my mothers room. There was a curtain drawn in front of us, concealing the sight of the bed where she had laid. I grabbed the curtain and violently slung it away, revealing an empty bed.

I fell to my knees, shaking in disbelief.

"No!!" I shouted. "No!!!!"

Stark tried to reason with me, rubbing my shoulders to comfort, but I fought him away.

"Don't touch me!" I yelled. "Don't you do that!"

He backed away at my refusal of his affection realizing that the torment of my mother's death was more than I could bear. I writhed in emotional pain on the floor, feeling the full burden of the failure to retrieve her on my shoulders.

"Where is she?!! Where is she?!" I cried.

"Liza?" I heard a woman's voice say from behind me. "Liza what's the matter?"

I turned around to behold my mom sitting in a wheel chair with a nurse pushing her. I turned to her, giving her the most enormous helping of love I possibly could with a hug that could have lingered into all of eternity.

"Why are you crying honey?" she asked.

"Mom, I thought you were dead! I thought you were dead! Your bed was empty!" I exclaimed.

"I just went for a walk. Well, a roll I guess," she laughed. "I'm fine honey. I woke up. We're okay. Issiryth sent us back."

"Yea," I laughed. "She sent us back."

The tears were streaming down my face as both the burden of sorrow and immensity of joy filled me up at the same time. This roller coaster of emotion had me in a whirlwind of ups and downs. Mom wiped the tears from my eyes and hugged me back.

"I see you brought your handsome fella with you?" she winked.

"Yea," I laughed. "Here he is."

I looked up at the nurse who she, herself was crying.

"When does she get to come home?" I asked.

"Tomorrow I think. If everything checks out," she smiled. "I'll let you two be alone."

The nurse let go of mom's wheelchair and turned to walk away from us.

"Sweetheart do you want anything from the cafeteria? I think I'm going get some breakfast," Stark asked.

"No, I'm fine," I replied not all together able to respond given the state of my emotion. He understood, nodding his head and moving out of the room. My hands wrapped around the handlebars of my mom's wheelchair as I moved her into the room and shut the door behind us. Mom tried to stand, but her legs trembled as she did so, causing her to tumble backward and plant her rump back in the chair.

"Easy now. Let me help you," I said steadying her back and

helping her move to the bed.

"I haven't used these in a while I guess," she laughed, slapping her legs with each hand. She slid up into the bed and looked down at my hand that wasn't quite ready to let go of hers. "Thanks for coming for me Liza."

"I will always come for you mama," I responded, lying my head down next to hers and scooting her over to fit the rest of my body in close. She stroked my hair as I held her.

"So, you're pregnant?" she asked.

"Yes...." I responded.

"Is it Bl---"

"No! Don't say his name. Please! Don't say it," I said quieting her lips with my finger.

"Okay," she said.

"It's Stark's," I said quickly as not to perpetuate her questioning as I lay my head back down on her chest.

"Yes, I see you're complying with Issiryth's request as well. Stark is the man I just met?" she asked.

"Yes, mama. Please don't talk about it anymore, okay? I don't ever want to talk about that place or any of the people in it again," I said

"Okay sweetie. It's all going to be alright," she said giving my forehead a gentle kiss.

As I lie there in my mothers arms on the hospital bed, many things went through my mind. I remembered how a love lost threw me into the arms of another man; a man who wanted to control and own me. He showed me many wonders and tempted me with his offerings, but through it all, I remained steadfast in my goal to retrieve the ones who mattered the most to me. Perhaps I was still love addicted, but at least I was addicted to the correct kind of love. I can't say for certain that I would never love Blane again, but at that moment I knew I had at least had the guts to stand up to him. The doctor came in to mom's hospital room with his clipboard much in the same manner he did when I awoke from my coma.

"Well, hello there ladies! Is now a good time to talk?" he asked.

"Yes, of course. Come on in," I said.

"Well Mrs. Ward. It looks like you're all clear to go home tomorrow, but take it easy. I'm going to recommend some physical therapy to get you back on your feet again. How does that sound?" he asked.

"It's great! Thank you so much!" she beamed. The doctor left the room again as I looked over to her bedside table and caught sight of an off-white card with gold lettering. My heart sank to the bottom of my stomach. Dare I allow myself to know what Blane had to say to me again?

"Mom!" I shrieked, grabbing up the card off the table. "Who gave this to you? Where did it come from?!"

She sat up in the bed, in shock of my outward display of disapproval, really not uttering a single word to me.

"Well?" I asked in confrontation.

"Sweetheart, I don't know where it came from. I just woke up. What does it say?" she asked.

"I don't know. I don't care what it says! We have to get rid of it. I'm never going back to that place! Not ever!" I exclaimed.

"Okay, fair enough. Just throw it away then Liza," she said.

I picked it up and looked at it. It had my name on it just as the other one had. My hand shook as I opened up the envelope.

"Don't read it Liza. Don't let him torture you. You don't have to go back unless you want to," she said.

"And what if he tries to take the baby?!" I asked.

"He can't do that Liza. You're the baby's mother. Just throw it away," she said.

My hand trembled as I held the card in my hand, trying to decide whether or not I should open and read it. My mother's concerned face said it all, that I should just let it go. So, with that, I ripped it into shreds, throwing it in the trash can next to the bathroom door in the hospital room.

"Go to hell Blane!" I shouted.

As I stood there over the broken pieces of our shattered relationship, I cried a little, but only in victory. I had finally conquered my addiction to the negativity that was constantly throwing itself in my face. I still wondered what was real. If life and death were truly anything like what we thought they were, but what I did know for sure was that family was forever. I knew I would go to the ends of the universe and beyond to save them. I looked at mom and smiled. She smiled back. We knew without words that this was the first day of the rest of our lives and I would be forever changed. ---The End.

ABOUT THE AUTHOR

LC Owen has enjoyed the gift of words since childhood. Her authorship began back in 2008 when she began writing children's poetry and picture books. Through many twists and turns in life, she learned that writing can sometimes take a life of its own. When a story came to her through a dream, she realized she was meant to write an entire novel for adults. She wrote The Islands of Sedania series and several short stories including Healing Time and Greener. She features up-and-coming authors on her podcast LC Owen Books where listeners can hear stories come alive with her voice narrations. You can keep up with her work (and other authors) through her website www.lcowenbooks.com. You can also catch-up with her through her YouTube channels where she posts her podcast episodes (LC Owen) and personal adventures (lowencope).